PRAISE FOR

KNOCK

"Rebecca provides an important framework for helping others succeed as you advance in your own career and reflects on her commitment to upskilling emerging talent and bridging the opportunity divide through mentorship, compassion, and mutually beneficial relationships."

—GERALD CHERTAVIAN, Founder and CEO of Year Up

"The Knock Method is a must-read for founders, budding entrepreneurs, and well-seasoned leaders who are interested in learning how to best leverage their networks to create meaningful and sustainable relationships. The stories highlighted serve as critical reminders that success and growth is built on failures, setbacks, and hardship. No matter where you are in your career, I strongly encourage you to soak up these learnings, which will allow you to open your heart and mind to authentic relationship building and a renewed sense of purpose."

—JENNA BENN SHERSHER, Founder of Twist Out Cancer

"This book nails it. Rebecca puts her finger on something so important but rarely laid out so well. Here you have a well-researched (and field-tested) framework on how to do it Perfect for marketers, salespeople, trainers, or anyone who wants to build more authentic business connections. Get your highlighter ready, and crack it open. And be sure to print page 20 and tape it to your wall."

—**ANDY CRESTODINA,** Co-Founder and Chief Marketing Officer, Orbit Media Studios, Inc.

"This book is full of good practical advice, learned through personal experience, and is, perhaps, especially useful in these remote working times of necessary social distancing."

—**MICHAEL LIEBERMAN,** Senior Policy Advisor, Southern Poverty Law Center; former Anti-Defamation League Washington Counsel and Director, Anti-Defamation League Civil Rights Policy Planning Center

"*Knock* is just what students and professionals need. It is not only a confidence boost that they can achieve great things, but it also builds a case for why our bodies, minds, careers, and communities depend on high-quality relationships. The stronger our ties with others, the more we can repair the world—together."

—**JANE E. DUTTON, PHD,** Robert L. Kahn Distinguished University Professor Emerita of Business Administration and Psychology and Co-founder of Center for Positive Organizations at the University of Michigan's Ross School of Business

KNOCK

How to Open Doors and
Build Career Relationships
That Matter

REBECCA OTIS LEDER

AN INC.
ORIGINAL

An Inc. Original
New York, New York
www.anincoriginal.com

This work is being published under the *An Inc. Original* imprint by an exclusive arrangement with *Inc. Magazine*. *Inc. Magazine* and the *Inc.* logo are registered trademarks of Mansueto Ventures, LLC. The *An Inc. Original* logo is a wholly owned trademark of Mansueto Ventures, LLC.

Distributed by River Grove Books

Design and composition by Greenleaf Book Group
Cover design by Greenleaf Book Group
Cover Images: ©iStockphoto/servet yigit, ©iStockphoto/penkanya, ©iStockphoto/structuresxx, ©iStockphoto/MARIOS07
Author photo courtesy of soona.co

Publisher's Cataloging-in-Publication data is available.

Print ISBN: 978-1-7360283-0-8

eBook ISBN: 978-1-7360283-1-5

First Edition

To those chasing their passion, to those who have yet to find it, and to those who are committed to helping others develop their careers as they build their own—those closed doors aren't barriers; they're the gateway to what's next . . .

CONTENTS

\ ' /

A NEW WAY TO KNOCK

When we connect thoughtfully, opportunities will knock

I n 2009, Jeff Aeder, a Chicago real estate investor, and his wife, Jennifer Levine, a lawyer, faced a tough decision. When their daughter was in the sixth grade, they discovered she had learning struggles including dyslexia and visual processing (difficulty reading and interpreting what she sees). Her middle school provided resources to help with her challenges. But after eighth grade, where would she go to school and get the help she needed? They searched for a local high school appropriate for students with learning differences but found nothing. Determined to find an answer, they met with secondary educators, neuropsychologists, and high school counselors and discovered, in disbelief, that Chicago, one of the country's largest and most prominent metropolitan cities, did not have a school with the expertise to educate college-bound students with specialized learning needs. Unbelievable.

"Why not?" they asked.

"No one's ever taken ownership of it," the experts said.

So, Jeff and Jennifer decided to do something about it.

For their daughter, and for other teens with similar struggles, they began the journey to create Wolcott College Prep,[1] the school that Chicago was missing. But they couldn't do it alone. They needed to ask a lot of questions, get help, build new relationships, and knock on the doors of many of their existing contacts to raise funds to make the school come to life. They would need to build a community to build the school.

Jeff and Jennifer began fundraising for the school in 2009, when the economy was in a recession. Their first meeting was with an affluent, philanthropic Chicago family, introduced to them through a mutual connection. The family declined to give a gift to the school but provided feedback, suggesting that they raise money from parents of students and alumni. Of course, neither existed, since there was no school yet.

Jeff was prepared for the rejections along the way. He was also determined—he knew their job wouldn't be done until they opened the school and had an endowment. He learned from this early rejection and rethought their strategy.

Here's what he and Jennifer did next.

Jennifer traveled the United States to visit schools for students with learning differences, meet students and professionals, and research what led to success. It became clear that they would have to build a private school to specifically help students who needed specialized learning, but one that was economically and culturally diverse.

Potential donors asked how Jeff and Jennifer would keep the school inclusive of students with varying backgrounds and questioned the amount of money that would need to be raised to support students who could not afford the full tuition. Jeff and Jennifer landed on answers—they would raise enough funds to accept any student who needed the school's resources, regardless of what their family could pay.

They focused on each donor on an individual level. Jeff and Jennifer were counting on a significant donation from one particular individual, a man they knew well. He was very charitable and actively contributed to his community. He rejected their initial approach. Another no, another disappointment. Jeff described this one as a "big kick in the gut." He continued to keep this potential donor updated on the school's progress anyway. Although there is a fine line between being persistent and annoying, Jeff's approach was to continue with the updates until the potential donor asked him to stop calling. Jeff tried a new angle each time, providing the potential donor with nuggets of value, including sending him an interesting article here or there that he might appreciate. When Jeff found out the potential donor was a baseball fan who dreamed of playing golf with Sandy Koufax, he leveraged professional and personal relationships to set up a tee time with Sandy and invited the prospective donor to join. He thanked Jeff but declined, saying he was busy that day and mentioning, "I never got over what Sandy did to my Yankees in '63." When Jeff went to the golf outing, he asked Sandy to sign a picture for the potential donor that said, "Tough luck, Sandy." Jeff framed it and sent it by courier to him the next day.

The potential donor called Jeff and said, "I think we're ready." Then he made an initial contribution to Wolcott College Prep.

When Jeff and Jennifer faced rejection, they got creative with new ways to show value to potential donors and to highlight the impact they could make on the future school. In his quest for supporters of the school, Jeff believed that if those he asked said no, it was because they didn't understand the importance of the school and the needs it would serve. He knew he needed to continue to explain the profound impact the school would have on future students and the community until others understood its value in ways that were relevant to them, emphasizing how their contribution could make a difference.

Jeff and Jennifer put the work in, even before asking for money. They found and bought the school building and finalized the architectural plans. This validated that they were serious, that they'd be accountable to their donors and students, and that the school was personal to them, with a child who was facing obstacles at and outside of school.

They garnered support from those they shared similarities with, appealing to individual interests. During the first fundraising campaign, Jeff approached a potential donor who was a trader and mathematically oriented. The donor gave a contribution, but it was less than Jeff expected. In his follow-up note, Jeff gave this clever appeal: "There is a 100 percent chance my daughter is going to this school. You say there is a 20 percent chance your child might need a school like Wolcott College Prep. Your contribution is a little less than 20 percent of my gift. So, I'm okay with your contribution being out of balance, but in the event that your child's needs exceed that 20 percent, then I expect you to keep the ratio more aligned. Otherwise, I'm subsidizing you and you're much wealthier than I am and you don't need my subsidy."

The man replied, "Your analysis is sound." As the chance increased that this donor's child would need specialized education services like Jeff's for learning differences, he kept his word and donated more money. Jeff crafted his message in numerical terms that his financially savvy contact could relate to and infused personality and even coy humor into his communications. He uncovered the donor's emotional motivations and tapped into the analytical thinking style he could relate to with ease.

When I first met Jeff, I had just become aware of a restaurant he had recently opened, and I asked him if running the eatery kept him up at night. He turned to me and said without hesitation, "No, I'm up thinking about the school my wife and I built." I knew instantly that connecting with others is effortless to Jeff. He is intentional with where he puts his time and energy, and he pursues endeavors with a genuine dedication to innovating and making the world a better place for those he will share it with for years to come.

Jeff is a natural giver, always finding ways to help others, and his career and reputation proved he would follow through on his and Jennifer's plans to build the school, which meant others trusted and believed in them. Jeff has sustained an accomplished real estate investing career, backing people and companies that have been successful. He is highly respected for helping and supporting others; when he needs help or seeks support, people know he is serious and honest and personally invested (financially and emotionally) in his endeavors.

Earlier in his career, Jeff helped another highly respected Chicago real estate investor during a tough economic time. Because of Jeff's dedication to helping others throughout his life, when he asked this fellow investor for financial support for the school, the man contributed more than $1 million, making him the second-highest financial contributor. Building rapport and giving to others are part of a long-term commitment Jeff has to interpersonal relationships. Over time, Jeff's character served as a foundation for trust and credibility when it came time to ask for support to build the school.

Jeff and Jennifer's efforts to build high-quality relationships and put in the work to prove the school's future impact were fruitful. They secured thirty initial donors, who each gave at least $100,000 because they bought into the vision and had personal experiences with kids who struggled with learning, even though only three of them had kids that would attend the school in its first year open.

Jeff reflected, "At the end of the day, I got in front of everyone that I wanted to. They haven't all said yes. I'm still talking to all of them, but you have to be patient and know when to connect and when to hold off."

Wolcott College Prep opened its doors in 2013 and now serves more than 120 students, with specialized faculty committed to teaching to students' strengths. It has been awarded a National Science Foundation grant and is recognized as a 2018 U.S. Department of Education Green Ribbon Schools award winner.[2] Tuition costs were $37,500 in 2012–2013, its founding year. Half of the students received financial aid from the school in the first year, subsidized by fundraising dollars. To support the school's mission of promoting economic diversity and based on initial research and feedback, students are admitted based on their interest in attending and whether the school can support their learning profiles, not based on a family's ability to pay. The school emphasizes creating an environment that supports learning differences so its students can connect meaningfully with what they are learning and can build the skills of self-advocacy, self-awareness, and self-confidence that are necessary to succeed in college and beyond. As proud as a school founder can be, Jeff said, "It is an unbelievable place."

HOW JEFF AND JENNIFER KNOCK

I had the pleasure of visiting Wolcott College Prep several times, once to teach networking strategies during their annual career week for students nearing graduation. When I had an opportunity to interview Jeff in front of the student body about how he brought the community together to raise funds to build the school, students' eyes lit up learning about how their school came to be. There is something so energizing about walking through the halls and seeing students excited to be there. How incredible to witness the impact of Jeff and Jennifer seeing a glaring gap in education for their own daughter, then filling that gap by establishing a one-of-a-kind school for her and for future generations of students. And one might argue that they built the school one brick and one relationship at a time.

Jeff and Jennifer's strategies fit a pattern I call The Knock Method. It's a deliberate way to develop positive, mutually beneficial long-term career relationships.

Jeff and Jennifer exemplify the impact we can make when we thoughtfully connect with others in a professional context, yet on a personal level. This book will serve as your guide to applying the five steps in The Knock Method as you develop your career.

The Knock Method is a deliberate way to develop positive, mutually beneficial long-term career relationships.

This idea emerged after I experienced and noticed patterns in professional interactions in my own career. I'm on the upper age range of the millennial generation (individuals born between 1981 and 1996), having graduated from the University of Texas McCombs School of Business in 2007 (Hook 'em!). Contrary to the misinformed and generalized bad rep that our age group has more than occasionally acquired for expecting reward and career growth without putting in the work, I was part of a driven and disciplined group of students at one of the top five undergraduate business university programs nationally,[3] where I studied marketing. My hardworking parents afforded me privilege and access to higher education, coupled with an emphasis on quality education and encouragement—thank you, Mom and Dad—which helped get me there, but so did my own hard work.

My classmates and I had our fun during the college years. But I was often finishing up calculus homework that was due by eleven on Thursday evenings, dubbed "college night,"[4] instead of out socializing to kick off the weekend early. Let's just say calculus didn't come naturally to me, so I could have been out with my friends had I finished earlier. But, guess what? Although I've never once used what I learned in calculus in my career, I made some of my best friendships during those study sessions. I also learned helpful skills from my on-the-job training at internships that I still apply in navigating the workplace.

In college, our business school put a lot of focus on preparing for interviews, creating effective resumes, and navigating the job search. But, after I graduated and my internship led to full-time employment, I was only two years into my first job when the global management consulting company I worked for went bankrupt during the recession. All of a sudden, my network of fellow students, faculty, and the career services team I had built in from my time at the university was no longer a primary safety net. The skills we had learned as students helped us stand out as students but not as experienced professionals in the workplace. I had to figure out how to leverage my existing network from the university and life experiences, and continue building it as my career path visibility became foggy. While I navigated these career challenges early in my career and landed on my feet when my employer got acquired by a competitor, my creative side started to take a more prominent role in my life.

After starting my blog, *TheRebeccammendations*, in 2009, I quickly immersed myself in the local Austin, Texas, community to learn about small businesses like restaurants and shops, then to write and publish stories about their founders. As my audience grew and I became connected with the local blogger community, I was fortunate to find myself on several media lists, receiving emails from public relations (PR) agencies and media outlets with invitations to preview events and offers to try menus, products, and services. They were seeking mentions of the brands and clients they represented on my blog. The influencer craze was in its infancy (hard to believe, this feels like it was ages ago), and bloggers were gaining credibility with their dedicated audiences, which made us ripe for promotional opportunities.

Soon, I was on the receiving end of many shallow outreach emails from PR agencies, often sent without any indication that they knew who I was or why I was receiving their message. They left me with this question: Did they spend time on my blog to familiarize themselves with my content and what my readers were most interested in? Did they read my About Me page? (Hey, I worked hard creating my own website!) Of course, I appreciated the opportunities that came to my inbox, even if I was on a circulated PR email list, but without putting in the effort to actually connect, they reached out with an empty hope that I would represent their clients' brands and present them to my hard-earned audience without an established relationship. I responded to people who took a more personalized approach because they set out to form a relationship; I could see the value of what they could bring to my readership and that I could bring to them. In these cases, I wasn't just responding to an email address; I was responding to the person behind it who wanted to engage on a human level. I attended their events so I could meet business owners and see, touch, and taste their products. I was receptive to opportunities where I could have an *experience* that would be authentic to write about on my site, rather than a shallow *exchange* of goods or website links without mutual interest or the promise of a substantial partnership. But the generic messages asking for me to promote other people's products on my site without genuine intention beyond a profitable exchange continued—and they still do.

Ironically, a couple of years later, I found myself working at a search engine optimization (SEO) agency with an outreach department. One strategy stood out to me among the many ways we helped our customers improve the visibility of their websites. Our company was pursuing client brand mentions online, reaching out to bloggers and website publishers like myself for digital currency that would turn into business—and dollars (cha-ching!)—for the agency and its clients. A typical industry practice at the time was preparing articles or images and sending messages en masse to a list of website owners and content publishers. It was a spray-and-pray numbers game to see if anyone would bite so the agency's customers would gain a mention. Our agency practiced a variation of this, and sometimes it worked.

I wondered if we were helping website owners' readers or if we were focusing on quantity rather than quality content for the primary benefit of the brands we represented. Were we adding value or simply looking for a transactional exchange, with requests that could come up empty after a tedious outreach effort?

As I observed this industry practice, I craved positive human connection with depth and greater potential for longer-term benefit for all involved. That's when I suggested that our agency develop a higher quality content marketing initiative to create richer stories, data-driven graphics, and compelling points of view on behalf of our clients—digital assets that website owners would find valuable and relevant for their audiences. It still wasn't building a unique partnership with each individual website owner, but with our customers and talent investing in this new practice, it was a start. And we gained more traction.

The unpersonalized targeting that I was subjected to as a blogger and the similar messages that the SEO industry had a history of sending are examples of agenda-driven outreach. It happens all around us in business and as we build our careers. Due to limited time and resources, it's easy to default to a quick copy-and-pasted message while going down a list of contacts, or to send an unsolicited resume in pursuit of a job, or to try the old "phone-a-friend," hoping someone can drop everything and give you what you need. (Those of us who have a handful of friends who will answer anytime we call are lucky, but they aren't the answer for all of our needs.) In a professional context, the quick "Hey, can you help me?" approach often comes in handy when we're in a bind, but can also come off as a low-effort way to look for a job, a mentor, an easy answer to a tough challenge, or a quick fix to a business problem. I've done it too. I've been so focused on a personal career goal that I didn't take the time to slow down and truly connect with people I could create partnerships with, instead of more mechanical "meeting needs" requests. And the result is low impact and disappointing, too.

While we can and should help others with favors and generosity (this is why I dedicated Chapter 5 to this very topic), genuine relationship building tends to get lost in the hustle and frenetic pace of life. We live in a world where it's so easy to communicate, and yet we look for quick, one-sided help in the form of a shallow ask and don't bother getting to know the person on the other end of the screen. We're so concerned with the problem at hand that we forget to ask, "How are you?" then listen. And if they're having a bad day, to wait for a better time to bring up the topic on our minds.

As Lady Gaga said in a press conference after the 2019 Oscars about the significance and relatability of the wildly successful and award-winning song "Shallow": "The unfortunate truth is that our cell phones . . . are becoming reality . . . I wish to not be in the shallow, but I am."[5]

Many would agree with Lady Gaga that we are living in a shallow time, when self-worth is measured by social media followers, influencer status is overshadowing human impact, and instant gratification is just a click away (hello, Amazon Prime

Now). Many of us are craving more—more genuine interactions rooted in reality beyond our cell phones, more true human connection, not only in entertainment and in our personal lives, but in our careers.

But, with this depth and substance in human interactions that is lacking, let's not be so hard on ourselves. After all, we're not taught how to establish high-quality, positive, mutually beneficial relationships—a deeper, more intentional form of networking. Classes and resources covering these topics aren't baked into our upbringing—no matter where we grew up—and when we get to a junction like a first job, a graduation, or a job change and need the skills to apply more thoughtful human connection, we don't know where to turn. A glaring gap in education and confidence exists among students and professionals navigating their own careers.

So let's fix that! I believed that there had to be a better way to open up doors so that opportunities "knock" for all of us.

I identified a problem we all face and set out to solve it. My behind-the-scenes experiences on both sides of the blogger-PR experience were representative of what I saw all around me, including what I experienced while navigating multiple job and career changes, managing cross-organizational programs within a global company, and starting a business. Two telling trends stood out to me about how we communicate professionally in this on-demand digital age:

1. We are focused on an exchange versus an experience

The typical outreach is a quid-pro-quo interaction, with a "what can you do for me?" attitude for a quick outcome. Many of the outreach messages from outlets looking for blog coverage looked the same for every target, as media professionals went down their email list in search of press. Those reaching out hadn't become even slightly familiar with my writing or audience. And yet, they were asking for a favor in the form of a feature and link on my blog.

Take the following message I received, in which there is no name in the greeting and my blog name appears in a different font (ahem, copied and pasted—could it be any more obvious?). They even mentioned a popular PR tool (Cision) that ranks websites and helps marketers choose which websites to target for their benefit.

Hey,

I was browsing your work on *TheRebeccammendations* after finding it on Cision and it looks like we speak to a similar audience. I wanted to reach out to see if our client, [client name], could be included in an upcoming feature.

We recently wrote an article on pairing chocolate and wine which you can check out here: http://www.[clientname].com/wine-and-chocolate-pairings.

Let me know if this or any of our other topics would be a good fit for *TheRebeccammendations*.

We'd love to be a resource for you and your audience.

Best,

While I was grateful brands were finding my site and reaching out, this request fell short. If they had taken the time to get to know what content I had planned for the coming months or asked what kinds of content my readers might be interested in, they would have learned that I write all of my own content and only promote products and services that I've tried and genuinely recommend. Of course, I could have asked to sample the product, but that wasn't offered outright, and this mechanical email didn't exactly scream "go after this opp!" to me. Sometimes the agenda is this blatant; often it's not. Either way, it bypasses the essential creation of a partnership or shared experience *before* zeroing in on a potential opportunity, and takes the form of a more transactional exchange—this for that. In other words, they "knocked" on my door with a very shallow request and ignored the person on the other side with the power to open that door and keep it open. The sender in the outreach email left themselves little chance to find out that I have a major sweet tooth for chocolate, and maybe we could have partnered in an even more impactful way like collaborating on a recipe or creating a taste-test experience for their potential customers, my readers.

In another instance, when I owned a business providing full-time marketing consulting for small businesses, a contact asked me to a casual lunch to talk about some business needs. If it went well, I'd provide a proposal for my services and they'd become a client. So I thought. He came to lunch with two teammates and used our time together to ask pointed questions about their business strategy, which I was not expecting. I felt ambushed or, at a minimum, misled. They thought they could buy my lunch in exchange for free advice. First, I was running a business where I provided business guidance for compensation, which included an hourly rate that far exceeded my $15 salad. What went sideways? It wasn't about money; my business purpose was to help businesses that were just starting out, including startups and nonprofits where big budgets were out of the picture from the get-go—and I wanted to help everyone but needed to have some business sense around it to make an income. As the meeting went on, it became clear that they had hoped to receive my services to benefit their team over lunch, and nothing more. Don't get me wrong—I provide creative ideas for friends and colleagues all the time. It's part of my nature and my marketing mind that I come up with creative solutions to all kinds of problems in conversations that span friendly and professional. I've even been given feedback that I give away too much knowledge for free that I should be charging for. But, in this case, my established business drove them to reach out for professional advice, which should have been compensated for.

From then on, I learned to set the expectation that to provide professional advice, I would learn about the business needs, provide a proposal, and then establish a formal working relationship. I would be invested, and so would they. Lunch would be worth everyone's time because it would be the beginning of ongoing interactions. The working relationship would be much more of a positive, productive experience, rather than an uneven and disproportionate and unexpected exchange of this for that, where the lunch was an end point instead of a beginning.

2. We are focused on competition versus collaboration

When I worked in SEO, our clients wanted their websites to rank high in searches online. As a consumer, when you search for something online, such as "best restaurants in Chicago," multiple factors go into which businesses appear at the top of the list—the links you're most likely to click on. Our agency represented businesses that were seeking brand mentions and links back to our clients' sites from bloggers like myself. More clicks meant more potential business and, ideally, higher profits. And more links meant more indicators to search engines that others found that site valuable, which impacted their reputation to those companies, and thus could get them ranking preference.

I paid special attention to the SEO practice known as "link building"—seeking a high quality and volume of links that point back to a site (combined with many other factors) to boost website visibility and rank on search engines, and ultimately generate sales online.[6] I'll point out that thanks to my experiences working at the SEO agency, I've learned that there is absolutely value in establishing links from credible websites to others, and some of this practice includes reaching out to contacts who have mentioned a brand but forgot to include the link, so a gentle nudge can help readers and website visitors. However, the pure nature of calling this effort "link building" versus "relationship building" or a partnership between a brand and a website owner shows how transactional it can be. An instrumental—or this-for-that—mentality emerges, one that fails to create opportunities to collaborate on impactful content that values human experiences worthy of writing about. SEO is all about competition over collaboration; after all, there's only one number-one spot on Google Search Engine Results Pages (SERPs). You might think, "Well, that's what business is about." *Knock* is my call for change. I believe, even in business and even in the age of automation and artificial intelligence, that we can achieve financial success, compete in a marketplace, and build a brand that stands out when we create a more substantial human experience. And we'll all feel better about it.

While some agencies and website owners take a less personal approach to this strategy because search engines like Google reward it, they might not give much thought to *why* these search engines reward it. Furthermore, they set the goal of getting the link pointing to a specific site, rather than of providing quality content featuring their brand to website readers—a more human-centric goal. (See Figure 1.)

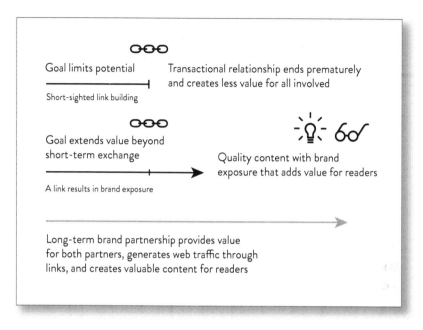

Figure 1—Extend the value of a partnership beyond a
short-sighted transactional exchange to gain long-term value.

Links serve as a referral, a recommendation, or a credible source of information. Similar to how you would give credit to a friend for their on-point restaurant recommendation or put more weight into a job candidate who is referred by a trusted colleague, links from one website to another serve as an indicator that search results content can be trusted. But the path to securing links doesn't have to be so transactional, especially if you intend to provide quality content to readers. When influencers and bloggers build rich partnerships with brands, intersite linking becomes a natural part of the partnership to bring valuable content to readers (outcome), rather than simply a means to an end (ranking higher).

Similarly to how the brands and agencies that get it right build a rich partnership with content creators or influencers, when you create a more human experience with contacts as you develop your career, you'll find that desired outcomes—trusted recommendations, respected reputations, and positive partnerships—may unfold more naturally, and the benefits are greater for all involved.

A SHIFT IN PERSPECTIVE

In 2014, after tuning into how professional communications skewed toward competition and transactional exchanges rather than collaboration and partnership with a focus on others, I began to look for better ways to go about networking. I was in the thick of a full-time job search for a new role in marketing. I noted what worked when I applied for jobs and reached out to connect with others professionally, and what others did that established trust and compelled me to respond to them.

What made people open to starting a conversation? What did I include in emails and phone interviews that seemed to capture the attention of busy, hardworking professionals? How could I differentiate myself from other candidates to make it through resume screening and secure an interview? I dug into psychology research and reached out to and interviewed successful professionals I admire who have built something new and impactful, or who have developed their careers through positive, high-quality, and mutually beneficial relationship building. Combining all of this experience, knowledge, and research, I created a handy and applicable way to generate and sustain those relationships in five steps: The Knock Method.

THE KNOCK METHOD

The Knock Method is a five-step framework for intentionally and genuinely connecting with others for mutual benefit as you develop your career. This book features supporting research to clarify *why* it works and stories from inspiring leaders about *how* it works in real-life scenarios to make a greater impact when put into practice. The Knock Method has been field tested in workshops with hundreds of students and professionals, and it has proven to inspire, educate, build confidence, and create powerful career connections that are still thriving.

KNOCK is an acronym for the steps, which are listed here alongside the elements that make them up in italics:

1. **K**now my topic, my contact, and specifics up front. Prepare to connect. (*Research/Specifics*)

2. **N**ot about me. Focus on my contacts, us, and our mutual impact. (*Other-Centeredness/Impact*)

3. **O**wn it. Be personal and authentic; invest in the relationship and the cause up front. (*Authenticity/Investment*)

4. **C**ommonality. Build trust to open the door. (*Commonality*)

5. **K**eep giving. Help others, and practice generosity and gratitude. (*Generosity/Gratitude*)

Throughout the book, follow along with this quick reference of The Knock Method that summarizes which steps relate to each chapter.

THE KNOCK METHOD®
Five steps to open doors and build career relationships that matter

High-quality relationship: A mutually beneficial collaboration where both parties contribute and the outcome is stronger

Know my topic, my contact, and specifics up front. Prepare to connect.	**Research/ Specifics**
Not about me. Focus on my contacts, us, and our mutual impact.	**Other-Centeredness/ Impact**
Own it. Be personal and authentic; invest in the relationship and the cause up front.	**Authenticity/ Investment**
Commonality. Build trust to open the door.	**Commonality**
Keep giving. Help others and practice generosity and gratitude.	**Generosity/ Gratitude**

For example, let's look at the amazing way that Jeff Aeder and Jennifer Levine built Wolcott College Prep. They did it by nurturing and fostering high-quality relationships with each and every supporter.

Here's how their approach relates to The Knock Method steps:

1. **Know my topic, my contact, and specifics up front.** They conducted research on their topic of how to build a school, and they got to know their contacts—their potential donors—on a deeper level, which helped them prove the value of supporting

the school and express it in ways their contacts could relate to. They gathered specifics about the amount needed to cover subsidized tuition, they bought the building in West Town, less than five miles from the Loop, and they secured architectural plans, preparing them in advance for questions so potential donors could trust the plans.

2. **Not about me.** They focused not on themselves, but on the impact potential supporters could make for future students and their own child. They illustrated the impact in terms that embraced other-centeredness, such as when Jeff used percentages for the mathematically inclined donor and when he related to the donor who was a baseball fan.

3. **Own it.** When they owned the fact that they had never built a school before, they practiced authenticity, as when Jeff mentioned his own child's needs in garnering support. They made an investment in the project and in relationships with potential donors by doing the up-front work to find the physical site for the school and creating plans to make it come to life, which let others know that they were serious about this effort.

4. **Commonality.** They found commonality with others whose children might develop needs the school could address one day, to establish trust and care, and open the door to conversations with potential donors and supporters.

5. **Keep giving.** By the time Jeff and Jennifer set out to build the school, Jeff had already built successful businesses and established a trusted reputation. They practiced generosity by bringing something of value to potential donor relationships and kept giving by building a school not only for their daughter's learning needs, but for students for years to come. They

followed up to thank each and every donor and kept them up to date on the school's plans in order to keep the relationships going with trust for the investment they each made.

Maybe you're not setting out to build a school, but whatever you have your sights set on for your own career, or even if you're still looking for what that next thing is on your career path, The Knock Method can be your guide to building positive, high-quality career relationships that may help your vision come into focus—or come to life.

MAKE IT YOUR OWN

Whether you're a *career grower*, like someone who's working to get to the next level at their current workplace; a *career changer* who is seeking and acquiring a new job or career; or a *career builder*, such as a high school or college grad just kicking off your career or a startup founder or entrepreneur making a new idea come to life, The Knock Method is for you. These are pivotal career milestones when it makes sense to boost the volume and quality of the relationships in your professional network.

Broadening and deepening connections that are full of potential, especially during these significant times in your career, will help you bridge the gap from where you are to where you might want to be. Nurturing positive, high-quality career relationships can help you land your first or your fifth job, learn about a new industry, find the right location for your new business, gain a mentor, move to a new role within a company, advance to a new level of leadership, gain executive buy-in for a new initiative, secure funding for a project, or assemble a new team. Beyond your specific career goals, these steps will help you learn how to strengthen and enrich the relationships in your professional network, both outside and inside company walls, by focusing on helping, giving, and contributing rather than simply furthering your own progress.

Who to use The Knock Method with

As you follow along with the steps in The Knock Method laid out in the chapters that lie ahead, you'll notice that I refer to your interactions with "contacts." A contact could be a person, a group of people, or an organization with whom you want to have an interaction or build and nurture a relationship. It might be a prospective startup founder, an existing mentor, a fellow student, a university alumnus from your school, a colleague or executive at your current company to pitch an idea, a future client, a professor, an author, a podcast guest, or even a potential employer. It might be an audience during a presentation in your current role at work, a partner organization, or a potential nonprofit donor. Anyone whose relationship is valuable to you—and even more so, that you think would be valuable to *them*—could be a contact using The Knock Method.

Make The Knock Method your own, and find ways to use it to elevate relationships in your own career network, no matter what path you're on or as you try to pave a new path. As you learn The Knock Method, think about the types of contacts you are nurturing relationships with right now, or potential contacts that you might seed new long-term relationships with as you develop your career. Dream big. Think about role models, leaders, and change-makers you wish you could connect with or meet to share ideas and forge new partnerships with. With the thoughtful preparation and the confidence you'll develop or reinforce through The Knock Method, anyone may be within reach. (Take it from me, every time I heard back from some of the prominent people interviewed for this book, I felt reassured—after my initial shock and surprise subsided.)

The Knock Method steps are not designed to be used in any particular sequence. Sometimes, you may zero in on one particular step, like sharing advice with a recent graduate who is a family friend (Step 5: *Keep Giving*). Other times, like when you're reaching out to interview a high-profile role model, you will find the power in combining steps: conducting extensive research about your contact's background, focusing on them rather than yourself in your introductory email, being authentic when introducing facts about yourself, and highlighting what you already know you have in common to build trust and open the door to a conversation (Steps 1–4).

How to think about
The Knock Method and timing

You can also classify the steps by when you use them. Use this second acronym to focus on *when* you're applying the steps—BDA: before, during, after. Ask yourself, will I take this step before, during, or after an interaction with a contact? For example, you will often research potential contacts to reach out to for an informational interview in your job search (Step 1: *Know My Topic and My Contact*) *before* you reach out or interact. You might also bring up what you learned in your research *during* an interaction, to show you prepared for the meeting. You might uncover a point of commonality (Step 4: *Commonality*) *before* you have an email exchange, share what you have in common *during* a meeting with them, and then follow up on some of your common interests in your thank-you email *after* you meet.

As you read on, refer to this handy tool whenever you need a cheat sheet on The Knock Method steps and how they might relate to the timing of your interactions with contacts. (See Figure 2.)

	Before	During	After
Know my topic and my contact	Prepare to connect by researching and learning about a contact.	Show how I prepared during the meeting.	Follow up using strategies and information from my research.
Not about me	Think about and bring to the forefront how my meeting could have a positive impact on the contact and others when I collaborate with them.	Focus on my contact, listen, and identify opportunities for their benefit and mutual benefit.	Follow up based on what I learned about my contact, and keep focusing on impact.
Own it	Invest, do the work up front, and be authentic when I reach out to connect with a contact.	Be confident in my own experience in meetings; reveal the investment that I've made.	Continue to shoulder the responsibility for maintaining the relationship.
Commonality	Uncover commonalities with my contact that will enable the connection and enhance trust between us.	Find ways to connect on shared goals, interests, and history.	Build on our commonalities by working on the relationship together. Each interaction creates more points of commonality that we can use to grow our partnership and value.
Keep giving	Help others as I develop my career; plant seeds that nurture new relationships.	Come prepared by already having ways to help others and solve their challenges as I meet with them.	Follow up by expressing gratitude; be generous now and in the future. Share resources and ideas after we meet that I offered up when we connected.

Figure 2—The Knock Method steps and timing.

TAKE IT OFF THE PAGE
AND PUT IT INTO ACTION

The power of The Knock Method doesn't stop there. How will you take what you've learned and put it to work in your own life? To help you take action on what you learn through stories, research, and the methodology within these pages, *Knock* offers practical tools and resources featured in the Appendix to give you a starting point, to guide you, and to help you stay accountable to yourself and others.

You'll find the following among other resources:

- 50 Informational Interview Questions

- 15 Questions to Answer before Reaching Out

- The Knock Method Honor Code for Building High-Quality Career Relationships

Whether in the workplace, while teaching personal branding classes, or as a mentor, I've heard questions like these:

- I want to reach out to someone who is more established in their career for advice, but what can I offer them?

- How do you network when you work remotely?

- I'm changing careers. How do I build rapport in the new industry when I'm just starting out?

- Where and how can I meet my first clients for my new business?

- How much time should I spend researching each prospective company or hiring team to prepare for an interview?

Knock includes actionable advice that addresses questions like these and how to create more meaningful interactions as you develop your career. It delves into why building positive relationships in our careers is critical not only for us, but for those around us as we pursue our own professional goals. Even more important, though, it taps into our innate human need to genuinely connect with others (and even our bodies' biological response when it happens or when it doesn't) as we contribute to the workforce, reach for our career goals, and make a difference in the world—together.

I'll be the first to admit that I don't have all the answers. I've sent emails before preparing enough, reached out to contacts too eagerly with a one-sided tone, and received rejection letters. I've also sometimes gotten what feels worse—no response—from inquiries, including interviews for this book. You can't get a yes from them all, nor should you expect to. (Think about it. If you heard back from every job you applied to, you likely wouldn't be where you are today, and you certainly wouldn't have learned as much on a frictionless path.) But you can still put effort and thought into how *you* approach relationships, and while others' behavior is out of your control, relationships are about much more than ourselves. The basis of The Knock Method is amplifying our consideration and fine-tuning our awareness of others in our interactions, and part of that is knowing that others have their own lives and priorities, and sometimes we don't fit into them. And that's okay. Similarly, as you'll read in Chapter 5, creating our own boundaries and priorities is key to building high-quality relationships and simultaneously building a fulfilling career. That's the beauty of relationships—people's lives are at the root of them, and when people converge at the right time, the right mix of experience, collaboration, and preparation maximizes what they can do together. Amid competing priorities and others' lives outside of work, I have been more successful at sparking someone's interest to open the door I knocked on with my outreach efforts when I used The Knock Method to connect more thoughtfully. I'll share how I did it in the chapters that lie ahead and provide simple strategies so that you can do it too. The Knock Method removes barriers like geography, variances in upbringing, organizational hierarchy or title, level of experience, industry, role, or which team you're on, to help you build, grow, and nurture high-quality career relationships on a human level.

By applying the five steps in The Knock Method, you can increase the chances that someone will open that door if you thoughtfully prepare, slow down, dive deep, and invest time in others and in the career growth opportunities that are worth it for them and for you. When you adopt The Knock Method as you approach new and existing relationships during your career, you'll find that you're knocking on others' doors more intentionally. And, by doing so, you will become part of a professional community that has an elevated quality of positive career relationships that may even come knocking at your door with exciting and unexpected possibilities.

WHAT'S NEXT?

In the next chapter, we look at the psychological research that proves that high-quality connections, specifically in a professional context, are good for our health—both body and mind. It will also touch on some of our self-imposed barriers to career development so you can approach career relationships with an open mind and get out of your own way.

Then, we'll dive into each of the five steps in The Knock Method, featuring firsthand stories and advice from professionals, founders, and leaders whose relationships fueled their success, including a food company CEO in Chicago, a mentorship expert who is the founder of a youth professional development organization, two nonprofit founders improving thousands of lives, an award-winning financial advisor, and a top legal counsel for a leading civil rights organization. I'll simplify heady psychology research about social interactions, relating it to the steps in a way that helps you understand *why* this approach is effective when you interact with others at work. Each step comes with a guide on how to put this method into practice, real email examples that opened the door to conversations that led to much more, and actionable tips to help you implement it in your own life and career. After the five "step" chapters, you'll find an appendix of resources and tools to help you before, during, and after interactions with your career contacts.

Knock is designed to be timeless, easy to follow, and quick to read, a book you will pick up and use more than once, and share with colleagues, friends, and family. After all, this method is about shifting focus off of ourselves and onto others to elevate our entire career network. Feel free to read a story, catch a quote, review the tips, or reference a resource, then put the book down until you find yourself preparing to connect with the next amazing someone along your career. In the end, you'll be inspired, learn how much high-quality relationships matter, get easy steps to follow, and gain practical tools that will help you take The Knock Method off the page and into your career relationships to make them richer, more impactful, and better—even healthier—for everyone.

HOW DO YOU FEEL
WHEN YOU KNOCK?

*Building positive career relationships
helps your health—body and mind*

This book is about much more than transactional, this-for-that networking. And the intentional networking approach covered within these pages goes way beyond the job search. The Knock Method is about building positive, high-quality career relationships that have a greater collective impact, and these relationships can take many forms. This approach and connective mentality can help you establish a long-term relationship with a mentor. It can lead you to finding a cofounder for your startup. It can result in securing a lifelong donor who believes in your nonprofit organization. It can even bring teams together within a large company, as you'll find in the following story.

PLAYING ON TWO TEAMS
WHERE EVERYBODY WINS

I faced a challenge at work. My employer, Salesforce, makes online tools that sales, marketing, and customer service teams use to run their businesses and connect with their customers. One such product is Sales Cloud, a system that helps sales reps track interactions with their prospects and customers to sell more effectively. My team within Salesforce's Customer Success Group was focused on helping our customers after they purchased licenses to use our technology products. We were creating helpful resources for customers; my manager asked me to find ways to display those resources *within* the product. Think of setup instructions and helpful swipe-left screens you might see right after you install a mobile app—this was the same concept. Once we did this, a customer who was logged in would be able to use this information to guide them while they were working within the Sales Cloud product.

Historically, we had distributed these resources through communications channels outside of the product, like email, which was an effective messaging channel, but it had some limitations. Some of our users may have signed up to use the product with a different email address from the one they checked regularly, so they weren't seeing our emails. They may have moved on to another job, so we could no longer reach them through their old email address. Because email wasn't a sure-fire way to reach and help all of our customers, it was time to explore ways to message customers more directly after they logged in.

My new assignment seemed doable. There was only one problem. My team didn't own the product or influence decisions about what messages were displayed within it; the product team did. Within our nearly fifty-thousand-person company, the vast product team was focused on building and maintaining our product, while my team's work was more in the realm of marketing and customer support. Our work rarely intersected.

I began reaching out to my team's contacts on the product team. I started out by asking, "How can we add our messaging to the product?" I didn't get far. Even though we were part of the same company, what incentive did they have to help us further our agenda when they had their own priorities? Their diligent product development work meant hustling to release new features three times a year, and I didn't exactly make a case for proving that slowing down or taking a detour would pay off. The responses I got were brief, and I wasn't making progress. One individual with significant responsibilities replied to my meeting invitation over email and said, "I really can't afford another meeting." After recognizing a pattern, that the doors I was knocking on remained closed, I had to change my approach. It felt like what Jeff had said about approaching potential Wolcott College Prep donors—if he got a no, it meant that others didn't understand the benefits of giving to the relationship. Like him, I needed to find another way to prove value. What was important to *them*?

I set out to discover it.

I shifted from a self-centered approach to one that focused on the product team's goals and the impact that achieving my team's goals would have on our customers, who were using the product. Instead of letting "no" remain a closed door from my busy colleague, I responded by asking questions that would help me learn, rather than just expecting to get something. I asked, "Is there someone else on your team you suggest I meet with?" and "Do you have a product development schedule I can get familiar with so I don't bug you during your busiest times?" Eventually, product team members introduced me to others who had more bandwidth, and I bookmarked their build schedule, referencing it so that I could be more sensitive and send meeting invitations that worked around their deadlines. I shared my team's goals, admitted that I was new to the product world, and asked for their team's help to understand it better.

The door had cracked open, but I hoped to open it even further because I could see mutual value. Through my research, I uncovered that 1) there was so much more to learn about the product team's landscape, 2) I needed to prepare better to increase the chances of having mutually productive conversations, and 3) the product team had no idea what we meant when we talked about "resources" customers would find helpful.

I needed to show them.

I created a categorized inventory of resources my team had developed that might be helpful to customers if they became more accessible by showcasing them inside the product, and shared it with the members of the product team. (I put it together quickly, so it wasn't pretty, but it worked to help them learn more about us.) I brought something to the table to show we had put in the work and we had intentions to help them and our customers. I gave them something to react to. We were no longer coming from what appeared as a needy, self-serving place and without any foundation to stand on.

The product team now felt motivated to review our list of available Customer Success resources because they wanted to ensure that customers had access to the most comprehensive list of resources possible while working within the product, and that what they were publishing within the product wasn't redundant or in conflict with what we were sharing through other communications channels. They wanted a consistent customer experience. *We* wanted a consistent customer experience.

Yes! We finally clicked!

We found shared interests and overlap in the goals our work set out to achieve. Through the learning lens instead of the "getting" lens, we also uncovered the areas that didn't overlap—areas where we could complement each other, rather than compete. With all of the knowledge I gained about the product team and how they developed new product features and vetted and published helpful information for customers in the product, I essentially became a representative of the product team embedded within our Customer Success Group. There were times when I was the sole advocate for the product team while in Customer Success Group meetings. I played for both sides. Why? I now understood that we needed to immerse ourselves in *their* world to even begin to have a productive conversation that was mutually beneficial. Of course, I represented our Customer Success Group in meetings that the product team began inviting me to so they could get a sense of our priorities too.

The best way to collaborate became clear.

It was not about furthering our own agenda and getting our stuff into someone else's territory. It was about speaking the same language (such as team-specific lingo), working toward the same goals, and pursuing mutual understanding and mutual benefit. It was about what we could achieve together—ultimately, more positive customer outcomes. We had two parts of an equation: one team dedicated to developing the best technology that reached our customers, and one team dedicated to helping customers

We needed to immerse ourselves in *their* world to even begin to have a productive conversation that was mutually beneficial.

through the most accessible channels, including our products. This was the beginning of a new, positive, high-quality, mutually beneficial relationship between two internal teams—including friendships among their members—within one of the most innovative technology companies.

As soon as the two teams began working together, we made the collaboration even stronger. The initial few of us who began the collaboration united both of our teams in a lunch-and-learn session with more than a hundred attendees, where we shared our plans, goals, priorities, and work processes. Executives leading each team presented and welcomed the other team, demonstrating buy-in and the value of our teams working together to our company and our customers. We began to cross-pollinate by having representatives of each team participate in the other team's efforts and share with their respective teams what they'd learned and what progress had been made. Eventually, we pooled our complementary skill sets and expertise to launch several initiatives together, like free learning apps and comprehensive trial experiences that have helped thousands of customers learn *within* the product, and we collaborated on the resources distributed there.

Two years later, both teams have come a long way, and our customers have benefited. The collaboration continues, as we share successes and insights in internal meetings and recognize team members who make an impact on customers through consistent collaboration. In fact, leaders across the teams are now invested in a tighter partnership to bring more valuable resources to customers within the product. If you're a Salesforce customer, you might see some of this goodness the next time you log in.

HOW I KNOCKED

I approached the product team from a place of curiosity and wanting to learn about their world. This allowed me to take a learn-first approach on behalf of my team, before defining the specific ways we could work with the product team. Contributing to the interaction early by bringing the list of resources my team had in our library is really what opened the door to a two-way conversation. I reframed my team's goals to be more aligned with the product team's goals and about how we could help customers together. We showed our dedication to collaboration, rather than just talking about it. Our work revealed specifics about what kinds of resources we were creating, and the product team was able to learn more about us. As a result, both teams uncovered gaps and similarities, established trust, and came to the collaboration in a way that put them on the same level. This approach also narrowed the gap between both teams so they could become more familiar with each other and, eventually, partners. Here's a summary of how the story aligns to The Knock Method.

THE KNOCK METHOD STEPS IN ACTION

Know my topic/contact **(Research)**	Conducted research on how the product team runs.
Know my topic/contact **(Specifics)**	Asked for specific details on the product release schedule and the best people to meet with on the product team. Also shared specific resources my team could contribute.
Not about me **(Other-Centeredness)**	Focused on the product team's schedule and needs.
Not about me **(Impact)**	Shared a list of resources with the product team, showing that our goals were to help our customers, not ourselves.

continued

Own it (Authenticity)	Shared a list of resources with the product team, showing that our goals were to help our customers, not ourselves.
Own it (Investment)	Admitted that I was unfamiliar with the product team's methods and used a learn-first approach, putting curiosity before asking for anything.
Commonality (Commonality)	Identified our shared goals to help provide customers with a consistent customer experience.
Keep giving (Generosity)	Continued to build on established trust and increased ongoing collaboration.

My story from work and the story about Wolcott College Prep showcase how The Knock Method aligns to real-world scenarios and the positive effects it has in a professional setting. Building high-quality, mutually beneficial, positive career relationships rather than transactional this-for-that networking generates positive outcomes. Working this way is good for our bodies, our minds, our lives, our careers, and our collective well-being and success.

Networking has historically been about *what* you want. The Knock Method approach is about *why*, and about bringing that forward in interactions with career contacts. Knowing why a partnership matters to a particular person and what impact you will make together makes all the difference. If your contact knows how to design websites and you know how to write website content, then the *why* is that you can combine talents to produce award-winning websites for digital viewers. If you know why a job at a particular company may be a fit with your experience, you can be more prepared to talk about how you can *contribute* to the company's bottom line in an interview. The purpose and potential of the relationship is much greater than a quick fix to a personal problem.

Instead of focusing on *what* you want to get out of an interaction with a career contact, think about what you can *give* to a partnership and why. Maybe you give your time to mentor a younger colleague and provide feedback on their first client project, boosting their confidence and making the client happier. Maybe you give through vulnerability, sharing your story about a personal medical struggle with

> **The purpose and potential of the relationship is much greater than a quick fix to a personal problem.**

a client who went through something similar and end up creating a support group. In fact, this approach of shifting the focus off of yourself and onto others and the impact you can make together takes some pressure off of you. It becomes less about what you're trying to accomplish alone with a lot of weight on your shoulders and more about creatively joining forces with others to help each other and make a bigger difference.

> **This approach of shifting the focus off of yourself and onto others and the impact you can make together takes some pressure off of you. It becomes less about what you're trying to accomplish alone with a lot of weight on your shoulders and more about creatively joining forces with others to help each other and make a bigger difference.**

Why focus on what you can give to relationships rather than what they can do for you? This approach—building positive, high-quality relationships—is actually good for your body and your mind.

As you learn how to apply each step of The Knock Method in your own career development, you'll gain confidence in how you're strengthening your community and its collective impact. As it turns out, you'll also be improving your overall health.

THE KNOCK METHOD IS GOOD FOR YOU

"Networking is fun!" said very few of us, ever. Unfortunately, traditional networking has put a bad taste in our mouths, and it's become an obligatory source of stress. We attend networking events where business cards are thrust into our hands by people who don't seem to care to get to know who we are. Or we arrive at a meeting and a business card is thrown on the table "just in case we need it" before we have a meaningful conversation. (I always found this a bit strange. You ended up at the meeting so you likely had their contact info to begin with, and also, that's like giving out your number before saying hello to someone—it's backwards!) We receive sudden messages for a quick job-related favor. We experience the expectation and guilt that we must immediately offer to do something in return when someone helps us out. When we work remotely, the limits created by physical distance create uncertainty and confusion about how to get and stay connected. Networking is often associated with job searching—a long, hard process that many people dread. (I've been there too.) And we often feel on the defensive when we receive a networking request because it feels so self-serving.

This kind of relationship, in the social psychology world, is described as "instrumental," or transactional, with the mindset of give-to-get or "what can you do for me?" Building relationships only to get something in return is shortsighted and often short lived. It also doesn't feel good and it's not as good for your health. It feels bad because it's bad for you!

Not having high-quality, positive relationships in your life can be detrimental to your health.

According to University of Michigan professor emerita Jane Dutton, PhD, coauthor of *Awakening Compassion at Work* and cofounder of the Center for Positive Organizations,[1] "What we should try to build are high-quality connections, and we should look at how we interact with others in ways that strengthen both people. It's not just about getting what you want—that kind of thinking will alienate us."

When we focus only on our needs and getting a quick pay-off, we may feel like we're connected because we are surrounded by people in our personal and professional networks, on social media, or in work settings. But, as Dutton said, when these relationships are transactional—in other words, not meaningful, mutually beneficial, or high quality—we can alienate ourselves and feel isolated. Especially in today's social media–fueled world where people feel the need to be validated by others, it's important to value people for who they are and not what they can do for you.

Especially in today's social media–fueled world where people feel the need to be validated by others, it's important to value people for who they are and not what they can do for you.

Isolation became a household term in 2020, as many of us were required to "self-isolate" to protect our health and that of others as the COVID-19 pandemic unfolded. Being physically isolated or feeling emotionally isolated can lead to loneliness, which is defined as when someone doesn't get the level of human connection they crave. And loneliness leads to a whole host of health risks.[2]

Did you know that a lack of meaningful connections and feeling lonely present the same health risks to the body as smoking fifteen cigarettes daily and present greater risks than alcohol abuse,[3] obesity, lack of exercise, and high blood pressure?[4] According to researchers at Brigham Young University, including Julianne Holt-Lunstad, a scientific research leader on this topic,

Did you know that a lack of meaningful connections and feeling lonely present the same health risks to the body as smoking fifteen cigarettes daily and present greater risks than alcohol abuse, obesity, lack of exercise, and high blood pressure?

loneliness contributes to a 26 percent shorter life expectancy,[5] and when you do have meaningful relationships, you have a 50 percent higher chance of survival.[6] One of the most relevant social work researchers of our time, Brené Brown, warns that not building high-quality connections and retreating, isolating, and denying loneliness causes fears and insecurities that occupy our mindspace and weaken our mental health. "This isn't just sad—it's actually dangerous," she says.[7]

In the book *Compassionomics*, Stephen Trzeciak and Anthony Mazzarelli examine extensive research that leads them to the following conclusion about human connection, compassion, and health: "It's not just the quantity of relationships, but the quality, that matters."[8] Vivek H. Murthy, MD, who served as the nineteenth surgeon general of the United States from 2014 to 2017, agrees. In his book, *Together*, he describes how after three years during his tenure in this role, he got to know people who suffer from all kinds of physical and emotional medical ailments across the country, and he saw that loneliness had become deeply rooted as an underlying and wide-spread health concern. "I've come to realize that social connection stands out . . . for addressing many of the critical problems we're dealing with, both as individuals and as a society. Overcoming loneliness and building a more connected future is an urgent mission that we can and must tackle together," he writes.[9]

If you can counteract loneliness for yourself and others by building high-quality relationships as you develop your career, thereby improving your health and quality of life, along with the health of others along your path, then this approach isn't a nice-to-have, it's a must-have.

What do you think? If you can counteract loneliness for yourself and others by building high-quality relationships as you develop your career, thereby improving your health and quality of life, along with the health of others along your path, then this approach isn't a nice-to-have, it's a must-have.

That old mentality about networking that makes you cringe? Throw it out the window. Leave it behind. When you think "networking," replace it with "mutually beneficial relationship building." Give it a try and say it out loud. You'll notice your approach will already slow down and have a more nurturing quality. Nerdy? Yes. Productive? Yes.

Making connections can be fun, rewarding, and good for you. Really.

Positive, high-quality career relationships have positive effects on you. They feel good, they're productive, and they lead to positive professional experiences. According to research from Jane Dutton and Emily Heaphy, a University of Massachusetts assistant professor with a PhD in management and organizations focused on the dynamics of work relationships, high-quality career relationships have rewarding and desired outcomes, meaning they turn out well.[10] You may have positive social interactions in your career relationships if you're part of a team at work where people support each other and help the company and its customers achieve their goals. You may have positive social interactions with a professional mentor who provides a safe space to talk about your career challenges while helping you succeed. You may have positive, high-quality relationships with work friends from past jobs with whom you keep in touch and share ideas, or meet up for lunch, dinner, or if you're of age, happy hour. (It's called "happy hour" for a reason, right?)

Positive career relationships may extend beyond office walls, geography, and years. For example, I had a positive career relationship with Ben, the owner of a high-end video production company called UPG Video, whom I partnered with to film introductory videos for small business owners in one day at an event we cohosted when I lived in Austin. We figured that even though Ben's rates were much higher than what my small business clients could afford, if we could film ten businesses in one day, each video at a lower cost, the day would be profitable, Ben's video services would get exposure for future business, and my clients would get a high-quality video at an unreal price. We would call it the Austin Video Marketing Marathon, and it was successful, helped everyone involved, and was so much fun! We would create mutual value for everyone involved in just eight hours. We just "jived" with each other, built trusted rapport, and got to know each other on a personal level. What was unique about this career relationship was that neither of us hired the other or exchanged money in a client capacity because we each served different clientele. The relationship wasn't transactional; it transcended each interaction, project, or event. It was a mutually beneficial professional career relationship with longevity. We shared the profits of the joint event, we made an impact for small businesses even though Ben's company often worked with high-end clientele, and we formed a true partnership that was less about our individual benefits and more about coming together and helping others. Over the past eight years, as I moved twice to different states, we've stayed connected long distance through social media, commenting on each other's updates. Whether I refer Ben's professional video production services to someone I know that needs them, or we partner together on a future video project, or we simply remain friends, our positive relationship lives on. I know that if I call him, he'll answer and we'll pick up right where we left off.

Combatting loneliness isn't the only health benefit of building high-quality career connections. What are some other ways positive interactions and relationships in professional settings contribute to our health?

Positive social interactions at work improve your physiological health[11]

Jane Dutton and Emily Heaphy cite research that proves that "positive social interactions at work have both immediate and enduring (positive) effects on the cardiovascular system like lower heart rate and blood pressure."[12] These effects vary based on the depth and length of relationships and the severity of stress involved. Relationships at work can affect how employees feel because people spend a significant amount of time there, and our work environment has the capacity to shape how we live our lives.[13]

We need human connection
to live a healthy life

Dutton believes we have a crisis of human connection in society. "I think a lot more about health than career success," she said. Maybe that's because a lack of human connection in career relationships—and in all relationships—is associated with many health risks. An absence or deficit of human connection and loneliness can triple fatal outcomes; weaken the body's immunity, as in susceptibility to catching the common cold; lead to a higher risk of heart disease and stroke and hinder recovery after a heart attack; and even affect genetics in how we express genes that circulate cells that fight off infection.[14] At the root of this phenomenon is the persistent stress loneliness puts on the body and mind, leading to inflammation and other harmful physical responses. So, when thinking about human connection as it relates to your career, it's best to pursue the types of relationships that *are* fulfilling and promote positive health outcomes.

The people you associate with have an impact
on your overall well-being

Have you ever considered how powerful it is to know which mutual friends you share with someone on Facebook, or your second- or third-degree connections on LinkedIn? According to authors Tom Rath and Jim Harter in their book *Wellbeing*, "Because your entire social network affects your health, habits, and wellbeing, mutual friendships matter even more. Investing in mutual relationships will lead to even higher levels of wellbeing. This is why it is critical for us to do what we can to strengthen the entire network around us. Simply put, we have stock in others' wellbeing."[15] Mutual positive human connections not only help us to be successful, but also contribute to our overall health.

Your mindset and mood might be affected by mutual friends, your colleagues, or your extended professional network

Your network, and the networks of those in it, shape how you feel. Rath and Harter explain: "If a friend of your direct connection is happy, the odds of your friend being happy increase by 15%—and the odds of you being happy increase by 10% even if you don't know or interact with this secondhand connection."[16] By strengthening positive and high-quality relationships at work, those who surround you in professional settings will also reap the benefits of connection, and they, in turn, will pass that benefit on, creating a positive ripple effect for everyone in that extended network. By building strong professional relationships, you are positively affecting your immediate network's contacts and having a far-reaching impact.

The health and wellness of those in your network affect your own health and wellness

The old adage of what goes around, comes around emerges when we work to build positive career relationships in our professional network. The more you give to your network and to the relationships in it, the more you'll get out of that community by simply being connected to those associated with it. If you help others, they may be more successful. If they're more successful, they may be more fulfilled. If they're more fulfilled, simply by having them in your network and being associated with them, your sense of fulfillment may increase. As described in *Wellbeing*, a Harvard study by sociologist and physician Nicholas Christakis reports, "People are embedded in social networks and the health and wellbeing of one person affects the health and wellbeing of others . . . Human happiness is not merely the province of isolated individuals."[17] Others you associate with contribute to your happiness, whether you're aware of it or not. And if you can be more thoughtful when connecting with those others, everyone will be better off, and most likely happier.

Positive, high-quality career relationships contribute to resilience

Dutton and Heaphy reference "physiological resourcefulness," which you can think of as resilience for your body. They describe physiological resourcefulness as "a form of positive health in which the body can build, maintain, and repair itself during times of rest and can more easily deal with challenges when they occur."[18] They assert that positive social interactions contribute to people's physiological resourcefulness by strengthening the cardiovascular, immune, and neuroendocrine systems—the neurons, glands, and hormones that manage and maintain how your body and mind function.[19] Who knew you could possibly strengthen your physical ability to bounce back from tough situations and meet challenges head-on at work by strengthening your career relationships?

WHAT'S HOLDING US BACK?

As you can see, building positive career relationships through ongoing interactions among people with whom we share mutual interests improves our health and has lasting effects on the well-being of our entire network. Why aren't we doing this more?

We just learned that it's good for our bodies—our physiological health—but what about our mental state? Fear and doubt can creep into our minds and limit us. Sometimes, we doubt that someone would take the time to meet with us if we have less experience.

Other times, we fear putting ourselves out there only to feel rejection and failure, worry that we're burdening someone, or believe that others may think we lack independence and can't stand on our own.

The Israeli psychologist Arie Nadler points out that we're caught between wanting to belong to a community and feel connected to others, and feeling like we can take care of ourselves through self-reliance.[20] This struggle hinders us from reaching out to connect with others or seeking help as we develop our careers. We all want to feel like we belong, which is why we yearn for social interaction, and this extends beyond our immediate family members to our communities of interest, friends, and coworkers.[21]

Nadler teaches us that as a result of relationships with those close to us, we expect and desire that feeling of belonging. And when we feel it, those close to us will help us when we need it, but we may feel some guilt that we need or expect their help. I don't know about you, but this research validates some of the contradictory feelings I experience when recognizing the need for help but hesitating before asking for it. If you feel the same way and are hesitant to reach out to others as you develop your career, that's natural! Fight your own resistance to asking for support—we all need it at times.

Regardless of our pull toward self-reliance, we should remember that reaching out to others and combining skill sets, experiences, and knowledge to build positive career relationships can help us tap into our desire to feel like we belong to something greater. And it makes others feel good to help us out. High-quality connections would rather help you and see you succeed than watch you flounder and struggle without help. Asking for support can help us to think beyond our own interests for a mutual benefit and improve our health in the process.

The Knock Method will help you build confidence and mental

stamina by having a trusted guide to approach relationships with a positive lens and a productive, collective purpose. Picture The Knock Method as a helpful friend on your shoulder or voice in your head that you can rely on to ensure that your fear and doubt don't hold you back from growth in your career and the possibilities that await.

KICK YOUR FEARS IN THE REAR

It's time to conquer the fears that could be holding you back. Here are some common questions rooted in fear and doubt that this book will help you conquer.

Is putting the effort into every interaction worth it?

Job seekers often doubt whether they really need to spend the time to write a unique cover letter for each job application—or even to include one at all. The answer is yes, if they want to optimally position themselves in the hiring process by allowing the hiring manager to get to know them, but even more so to show that they did their research and *can prove the value they'll contribute* to the company and position. Job seekers may copy and paste the same letter, replace the greeting and company name, and submit applications in bulk to a long list of possible employers. They doubt that going through the extra effort to customize each letter will actually produce a better outcome—in this case, getting hired for a job that is a good fit, especially in an age when job application systems are highly automated. Note: You are customizing the cover letter and application for *them*, the hiring manager and hiring company, to bring value to *them*. It's the first step in shifting focus from yourself to a contact, hiring manager, or company. As I recounted earlier in "A New Way to Knock," this quick go-down-the-list type of approach is also what the PR representative from the chocolate company did when he reached out to me as a blogger. Sure, this approach can be efficient, but it can also fall short. It can lead to missed opportunities beyond the job—these individuals and companies could become a part of your professional network for years to come, hired or not.

For example, I once formed a professional friendship with a hiring manager who didn't hire me. Even after I spent a significant amount of time preparing for an interview presentation and felt like I connected with the team, I didn't get the job. But I reached out to the hiring manager for feedback to improve my interview skills for future pursuits. Fortunately, she took the time to explain that my level of experience was more advanced than the job they were looking to fill, and her team didn't have financial resources to make many of my advanced marketing strategies come to life. Since she was also a collaborative person who thought beyond the job interview interaction, my interest in improving and my questions for her led to a series of conversations about our career and personal interests. We discovered that she lives in the city where I went to college and where my family lives, so I visit often. We meet periodically to share personal updates and career challenges. It seems hard to imagine, but it is possible to stay in touch with recruiters and hiring managers after applying to jobs that don't pan out. Long-term relationships won't always emerge, but it's up to you to at least try to connect more thoughtfully when you see opportunities for mutual value, because there's so much more potential when you consider the person on the other end of the phone or interview, and shift focus off of yourself.

Another time, I reached out for an introductory meeting with a colleague on another team at work because I was interested in an open job on his team. Instead of approaching the meeting by asking about the open role out of the gate, I opened up a broader level of conversation to get to know his professional background, his description of the team's responsibilities, and the projects he was working on to see if I could find ways to help him. I also shared more about my history at the company and the projects I was working on so he could get to know me. As a result, I built a bridge with another team and we identified ways we could help each other going forward. From the information he shared, I was able to determine that the team and role weren't actually the fit I was looking for, even without asking about it. We opened the door to a long-term relationship, however, instead of executing a short-term interaction that could be described as simply a means to an end . . . a dead end, perhaps.

A better approach to job hunting is to spend time researching each company or hiring team before an interview to get to know them on a human level. Uncover the job opportunities where you can make the biggest difference for *them* and highlight why your skill set for specific roles has the most potential for *them*.

Slowing down to be more intentional can help you filter which jobs may *not* be worth pursuing. Focus on quality rather than quantity and be helpful for others, rather than self-serving. Don't forget, companies want to hire great talent, and they're hiring so they can be successful. It's not just about you getting a job, any job; it's about finding one where you can learn and contribute, and they can learn from you and excel with you in the role. Think beyond a single interaction, and you may find the courage and stamina to put in the investment to pursue individual opportunities and relationships with a higher level of effort and quality.

Why would someone with significantly more experience meet with me? What can I bring to the table?

While from the outside, it may look like successful people progressed in their career because it came easy or naturally to them, they likely got to where they are with the help of many others. Success is not a one-woman sport. Leaders pave the way for others because many helped them, they're in a position to do so, and they have experience others can learn from, or they feel the desire to lift someone up. Also, people who are in a position to help others may find it easier to do than someone just starting out might. For example, a business leader may be able to help hundreds of students by recording a presentation that can be accessed online, on demand. This may be a simple effort for the leader, who has a lifetime of experience and can deliver a message they know like the back of their hand, but for someone early in their career, it might be a significant task. Professional experience lends itself to helping others with ease. Let go of this doubt that those who are a few—or many—steps ahead in their career wouldn't take the time for a productive conversation. This can and does happen, but only when you help the other person to help you. Make it easy for them to meet with you. Go out of your way so they don't have to. Think of ways to help a leader you're looking to connect with. Gerald Chertavian, the founder of Year Up, whom you'll hear about in Chapter 5, suggests saving a leader's time by grabbing them coffee or lunch before you meet (maybe ask for their go-to order first), or recommending lunch spots close to them to minimize their travel time. Create an experience with the other person, rather than expecting it to be an equal exchange.

When you're intentional about how you connect with others, it becomes clear that the time you spend together is mutually valuable, rather than a scenario where you are taking advantage of someone's expertise. By using The Knock Method and the mentality that accompanies it, you can learn to shift the focus from yourself to your connections and the impact you can make together.

Approach relationships with generosity. You will prove to leaders and established colleagues that spending time together is worth the time and mutually beneficial. When you prepare to connect with others and think beyond your own goals, others will consider making time for you a delight, not a burden. We all have something to learn from each other, no matter where we are in our careers or lives. Mentors learn too. Teachers learn too. Executives learn too. According to Julie Smolyansky, CEO of Lifeway Foods,[22] "Every relationship is both learning and teaching; you're both a teacher and a student/learner in every case. Even when I'm the mentor, I'm a student. When millennials ask me for things, I'm learning from them too. It should be a mutually beneficial relationship, mutually helpful."

No matter your vantage point, if you demonstrate positive intentions, express genuine interest in others, and dedicate time and attention to others' lives and work, investing in an interaction with you will be compelling and exciting, and everyone will win.

How can high-quality relationships possibly emerge if I work remotely?

All five steps in The Knock Method can be put into practice from a distance. People who are successful at building positive, high-quality relationships don't see distance as a barrier and often use technology to overcome it. Different perspectives bring about powerful partnerships. Collaborating across cities, states, or continents can have a broader impact because by coming together, you can widen the community you are building. Handwritten thank-you notes or gifts sent through the mail enrich career relationships.

Buying someone's book, whether shipped to your doorstep or downloaded on your digital device, shows you've invested in and are interested in their work. Traveling to

People who are successful at building positive, high-quality relationships don't see distance as a barrier and often use technology to overcome it.

conferences or connecting through digital platforms shows you've put in the time and effort to learn from and share ideas face-to-face with others. You may have to work that much harder to get to know someone or pursue a job opportunity by building connections at hiring companies from a distance, but you can do it, and the chapters coming up will provide a blueprint. The story I shared about how I helped bring two internal teams together at Salesforce took place exclusively remotely. I had the opportunity to meet my own team members and the product team members in person a few times during work trips, but most collaboration took place through email, phone calls, video calls, and online collaboration tools in the cloud. Use creative ways to connect with others, including social media and mobile apps. Be flexible, adapt to the ways *they* prefer to communicate, truly listen to understand *them*, and work around *their* schedule so you can tap into their world and show how you value them. While there's no replacement for live, in-person interactions, the power of connection between individuals, groups, and teams bypasses time zones or physical presence. You can knock on doors (thoughtfully) from almost anywhere, and you'll see that others will answer.

So, you can address these common fears and diminish these doubts when you broaden your perspective beyond the career challenges ahead of you and focus on the big picture. Think of yourself as an important member of your broader community who can make a significant impact on others' health and well-being and your own health and well-being. The Knock Method will help you build confidence through the research-backed steps and stories that strike a balance of grit and meaning that can lead to richer connections across your existing and future network. Now that you're equipped with scientific insights that help you understand the effects that building positive, high-quality relationships can have on the body and mind, let's get to the first step in The Knock Method: filling knowledge gaps about who and what you're headed toward through research and preparation as you develop your career.

\ ˈ ⁄

1

KNOW MY TOPIC
AND MY CONTACT

Prepare to connect through
research and specifics

Building effective, positive, high-quality career relationships is only possible when you see someone else's time as
valuable. You don't often get useful time with others, and
the supply is not limitless. You may get only *one* chance to turn
a single interaction into something more. When you give time to
another person and they give time to you, you can combine your
unique professional and life experiences, brain power, human
networks, education, and perspectives to benefit each other, and
even partner to go beyond yourselves and help your community
too. The power we have together is powerful.

Once you see someone else's time with you as precious, rare,
and full of potential, your goal should be to make the most of it and
spend it wisely. Don't make it about you or spend it asking questions
you could easily find the answers to on your own. Make it mutually

beneficial. Make it worth *their* time. Do them the favor of doing your research before you use up their limited, valuable time.

To prepare to connect with someone new, you need to learn about them *before* you connect with them. How else would you know you want to connect with them in the first place?

This is the first step in The Knock Method: *Know my topic and my contact.* This step focuses on research, on having specific details at the ready, and on how to prepare to connect. It functions as a filter, weeding out irrelevant opportunities and conversations that not only waste others' time, but also hinder your own progress.

Research gives you a head start and saves others' time.

Research gives you a head start. It puts you ahead when connecting with others because you can avoid wasting time on facts that could have been uncovered either online through public resources or through a mutual contact ahead of time. Odds are, you're reaching out to a particular person because you already know something about them.

Before your upcoming meeting, do you have any background information about the person, and do you know specifics about your topic?

Have you gathered baseline information about them in advance, such as the city they live in, their time zone, the nature of their work, their role and tenure with the company they work for, or their activities and interests? You can research these topics using their social media posts or profiles, the "About Us" information on their company website, or news articles about them. You can use this information to relate on a personal level—maybe you visited a favorite restaurant or park in their city. You can propose meeting times in their time zone to save time, rather than going back and forth in your inboxes trying to find a time to connect (who doesn't like fewer emails?).

You can use what you know about their work to craft productive questions that uncover less available information about their current challenges, how they spend a day in their role, or what they find most rewarding, rather than gathering basic facts you could have researched ahead of time.

- **Have you prepared questions in advance to guide your conversation in productive directions?** Have you shared an agenda of topics you hope to address during the call? Do you have details like pricing and timelines in your back pocket in case questions come up? If not, you may not be ready to meet just yet.

- **When you prepare, you're putting yourself, and them, at a huge advantage because your shared time is about to be that much more productive.** Set yourself up for success, and set them up for a meaningful interaction with you that can lead to a standout conversation, rather than just another get-to-know-you phone call.

Once, before meeting with a director on another team where I worked, I asked a colleague about the director's personality and his current work priorities. Although this was my first meeting with him and it was intended to be a basic introduction, I had an idea for a specific partnership in mind. My colleague mentioned that the director values when people have a well-thought-out plan before meeting with him, so I developed the project plan and was ready to present to him when we met

> Set yourself up for success, and set them up for a meaningful interaction with you that can lead to a standout conversation, rather than just another get-to-know-you phone call.

in case the conversation went in that direction. In this case, I prepared to connect twice in advance of the meeting: 1) by asking our mutual colleague about the director and 2) by crafting the plan. The conversation was much more rewarding for both of us; based on my colleague's insights, I was prepared with specific answers for the director's questions. Because I did the research to uncover his expectations and also did the prep work, we got my proposed project off the ground shortly after the meeting, rather than spending time afterward going back and forth on project plans. I started off with how I could help him achieve his goals through my own contributions, rather than how he could help me, and jumped right to the ways we could help each other.

Preparation like this could change the path of your career and even make an innovative idea come to life at work. Here's what happened when a training expert doubled down on preparation before pitching a new idea to an executive at her company.

THE POWER OF PREPARATION BEHIND THE PRESENTATION: WINNING OVER AN EXECUTIVE WITH A NEW IDEA

Erica Kuhl had a brilliant idea for her company, but how could she make it come to life?

As sales became more technical in the early 2000s, sales operations staff—those who make sales processes more efficient—often ended up with an extra job. They had to meet company and market demand to become a system administrator (sysadmin) responsible for setting up, managing, and maintaining the company's internal technology systems. Part of Erica's job was to train hundreds of sysadmins who worked at their customers' companies. "For four or five days, I poured knowledge into them. They absorbed it and connected with other people from all different industries and all over the country," she recalled, "and then they had to go back to their companies to do this new, specialized role, and they were alone." She began to wonder if there was an opportunity to bring them together, virtually. She asked, "Why isn't there a place for them to connect after they come to the class to bounce ideas off of each other or share?" She began formulating a solution.

After considering this for years, Erica found herself in a position to pitch her boss, the chief marketing officer (CMO), on her idea to create a digital community where sysadmins and others in tech roles could meet, connect, and share challenges and ideas. The CMO "was a brilliant storyteller and a whiz at PowerPoint," she recalls. "He even used to teach classes on how to create compelling presentations in PowerPoint." So she knew she'd have to create a top-notch PowerPoint presentation for her pitch. It would have to include concrete data, because he was a data guy, too.

She wanted to prove there was a need for this program, and that she had the track record to lead it successfully. Here's how she prepared.

"I gathered as many facts as I could on why this would work—the number of admins I had taught, the increase in number of students in the classes because of the program's effectiveness, and the limited resources used to grow the successful program," Erica said. She filled her PowerPoint presentation with as much detail as she could, including plans for the new digital community program. She included her recommendation for success metrics so that she had the answer to the inevitable CMO question, "How will we know if this program is working?"

Then she set out to master the medium. Erica's expertise was in telling stories, not PowerPoint. She thought, "I need to nail this." She vetted her presentation through others at the company who had PowerPoint expertise and had them role-play the CMO, anticipating his questions and giving feedback they expected him to give. With her extensive preparation and her proven experience with the training program, she was confident this digital community program would work.

She went to the meeting and presented her idea to the CMO. And failed. His response was, "This is a bad idea." Erica recalled, "I was shocked because I thought it was brilliant."

But she knew there was proof that this program would add value for their customers, and she was committed to her idea as a solution to a problem. Erica didn't accept no as an answer. She came back to him and said, "I really think this is a good idea, and this is why." She pointed out all of the data she had gathered from past experience to forecast the numbers for the concept to prove it would work.

He said, "You've been here five years; you're a good performer. Why don't you give it a try, while you keep going with your current responsibilities too?" He gave her a chance to develop this program as a side gig, and she seized it. "That's a win; it's not a no," she said.

What convinced him to give her a shot? Erica said, "I never really asked him but proved it instead. It was the up-front work I did on the PowerPoint presentation. I didn't go into the meeting with fluff. I knew what he wanted [data] and what worked for him [a strong PowerPoint]." Bringing him a compelling story in a medium that he liked was a key reason he decided to give Erica a chance. Knowing the likes and dislikes of her primary contact and what resonated most with him resulted in a successful pitch. But now, the real work started—she had to prove she could follow through on her idea.

The CMO allowed Erica to use an existing company website

that at the time hosted event resources. She learned HTML and found creative ways to create a discussion forum for the admin community members and a blog with resources to help the community. And it started to work. "I knew I had to show value to him quickly because otherwise, I'd lose the opportunity immediately. I had something up and running within about six months," she said.

As of 2020—twelve years since it began, her little project is now Salesforce's massive digital Trailblazer Community made up of three million online community members across twelve-hundred-plus community groups in ninety countries with more than three hundred monthly meetings.[1] And it exists, in part, because Erica prepared so diligently for her meeting with the CMO.

HOW ERICA KNOCKS

Erica doubled down on preparation before her big pitch. She had to do the groundwork before the meeting, not only to gather the details from the success of her previous training program, but also to learn about the CMO and his affinity for the PowerPoint format and data. Even when he said no, she went back to him with proof that her program would work because she had done her research and presented specifics, like how and where the community would be managed, that led to his approval for her to give it a shot. Here's how Erica's approach to gain executive buy-in aligned with Step 1: *Know My Topic and My Contact.*

THE KNOCK METHOD STEP 1 IN ACTION

Know my contact (Research)	Received feedback from colleagues who knew the CMO and knew his preferred presentation style.
Know my contact (Specifics)	Delivered a sharp presentation in the CMO's go-to format, PowerPoint, and focused on data, which he valued.
Know my topic (Research)	Even after hearing no, compiled details about previous training program success to prove likelihood for the new idea to succeed.
Know my topic (Specifics)	Prepared a detailed plan with specifics of how and where the community would be managed, identifying success metrics to track progress. Preemptively answered questions to reduce doubt and overcome rejection.

Knowing your contact and your audience isn't just for career advancement. It also comes into play for sales scenarios. Here's a story that shows the difference you can make in the lives of others when you prepare to connect through research and roll up your sleeves to dig into specific details prior to professional interactions.

AGE IS JUST A NUMBER:
HOW ANTICIPATING CUSTOMER NEEDS
AND UP-FRONT RESEARCH PAYS OFF

Could you sell a life insurance policy to a seventy-six-year old? Rick Otis did.

Every morning, a group of six or seven Jewish men would sit around and kibitz (chit chat) at the International Bakery in El Paso, Texas. It was the twilight years breakfast club. Rick noticed them.

Rick, decades younger, was a CPA and a new MassMutual financial advisor. As he recuperated from recent cardiac surgery, he regularly stopped by the bakery for a heart-healthy bran muffin. One day, Mr. K, whom he knew from the community but not well, invited Rick to join the group. He was an impressive seventy-six-year-old man, who among many life experiences had survived the Holocaust. After about six months of Rick's being in the "in crowd" at the bakery, Mr. K. gave him a call.

"My CPA says I need more insurance, but he doesn't think I can get it," Mr. K said. "I'm gonna give you a chance. I don't know if you can do it, but I'll give you a chance."

Insurance companies determine whether someone can buy a life insurance policy based on the individual's health status. If the person is in good health, they're at a lower risk for costly claims. But depending on the severity of their health conditions, the premium may be astronomical, because the risk is higher. Mr. K had some health challenges, as most would at his age.

As he learned more about Mr. K's medical situation, Rick thought, "This will not be easy." He wanted to help him, but this was a high-stakes, high-value policy. If he could get Mr. K insurance, the premium would be about $80,000 per year.

"It was a huge premium to sell," he said. Rick called his company because he didn't even know if he could sell a permanent policy to a person of Mr. K's age. They approved, provided the policyholder would get an exam with one of the insurance company–approved medical doctors. With Mr. K's permission, Rick contacted Mr. K's regular doctor, got a sense of his medical history, and arranged an exam with the insurance company–referred doctor. After one month, the insurance company approved Mr. K's policy but at an expensive rate, as expected. As Rick explained, "I thought, there's no way he's going to buy this. I even scoped out the competition for a price comparison and found that their policy would cost $6,000 less annually."

Rick met with Mr. K and explained that he could get him coverage, but only at a high premium rate, due to his medical history and age.

As Rick had anticipated, Mr. K asked about pricing at other companies. "Since I had already prepared for this scenario, I told him what I learned through my research, that he could save by going with a competitor," Rick said.

Mr. K said, "MassMutual is a better company, and I'll go with them. Go see my secretary and she'll have a check for you."

Rick, still with surprise in his eyes, shared the impact of this effort. "In that year, I won an award because of the value of that policy." His relationship with Mr. K extended far beyond the policy and turned a valued business relationship into a personal one that has lasted more than sixteen years, and still counting. Rick leaned on Mr. K as a mentor and friend as well.

HOW RICK KNOCKS

Rick's approach to building positive relationships is unique, personal, and characterized by extra effort up front and at every step of the way. He's successful because he gets to know prospects and clients on an individual level and anticipates their needs, often before he meets with them. He prepares to connect by doing his research to get specifics like pricing and verifying a client's eligibility for an insurance policy, even if that means finding a competitive offer that could risk a sale for him. He goes to great lengths to help others and prioritizes values like privacy and the well-being of his clients and friends, as he did when he asked for permission to reach out to Mr. K's doctor. He listens for cues that will lead to opportunity and asks key questions that prepare him to bring beneficial ideas, rooted in statistics and facts, that can help his contacts most effectively. He prepares to connect thoughtfully, and it pays off. Rick has that *je ne sais quoi* that makes it almost effortless for him to open the door with others, and keep it open. In fact, if you go anywhere with him, he'll literally open the door for you.

I'm grateful to have learned about the value of relationships from Rick, especially because he's my dad. Far beyond his natural ability to sell, he has taught me about the importance of greeting strangers with a smile, asking how someone's day is going, or changing it by sharing a compliment, and that it's more about human connection than winning in business. His natural ability to be open, share advice, and break down barriers between people—personally or professionally—with a laugh is a treat for those, like me, who get to witness it firsthand.

Here's how Rick prepared to help Mr. K:

THE KNOCK METHOD STEP 1 IN ACTION

Know my contact (Research)	Asked Mr. K for permission to contact his doctor to set up medical testing.
Know my contact (Specifics)	Got to know Mr. K on a personal level and learned his unique situation, including age and health history, to help serve him better.
Know my topic (Research)	Contacted his employer early to find out if Mr. K was eligible for a policy, and at what cost.
Know my topic (Specifics)	Proactively contacted a competitor to compare rates in anticipation of Mr. K asking.

KNOW MY TOPIC AND MY CONTACT: THIS STEP IN CONTEXT

If someone calls you for advice about applying for a job at your company, it's hard to believe when they start with "So, how long have you worked there?"

Didn't they look it up?

This has happened to me. A student from a class I taught contacted me on LinkedIn, where my career history was clearly accessible. During our scheduled call, it became clear he didn't prepare relevant questions and had not even checked out our company's website for recent news and updates.

It's natural to not assume that everything you read about someone is the most current or accurate information, and you could say something like, "I think I saw that you've worked there for five years, is that right?" But this call seemed to start without any prep work as a basis. I was surprised that he hadn't prepared unique questions before we spoke, similar to how I was taught to bring a list of questions to an interview.

If he had started with a foundation based on research, he could have used our time together to ask for highlights from my employment with the company, examples of how I made a difference with customers in my role, or information I could share about the work my company does in his specific industry, which could put him ahead in interviews. I would have also learned more about him, like which aspects of the job or company interested him the most, or some of his career goals or personal interests, which I could have passed on to a recruiter when referring him for the role.

Conducting research could have helped me help him better.

The best way I could help him was to recommend some ideas for researching our company so he could be better prepared for possible interviews, and I set him up with a colleague in his industry so he could get a better feel for that team and opportunity. I wanted to help him become more prepared for a more focused job search. While I hope my advice helped him, I believe he could have maximized our time in a more productive way for both of us had he prepared to connect with me.

When you prepare before you connect with others as you start, build, or grow your career, you prove that you're prioritizing the person you're contacting and the related opportunity. It shows that you put in the work because you value their time. It helps you gain knowledge and boost your expertise, what I call in Chapter 3, making an investment in an opportunity or relationship. This knowledge can further validate that an opportunity or relationship is worth contributing to, or it may even reveal that you were about to pursue an opportunity or spend energy reaching out to someone who isn't the right fit, which avoids wasting everybody's time. It accelerates your progress because it helps you shape the conversation so you can focus on specifics they're likely to be interested in, rather than general discussion that doesn't help either of you very much. It helps you gauge what's going on in someone's life, which may guide the timing of when you decide to reach out, and helps you make your conversation more personalized and interesting to them.

For example, you may decide to wait until your contact is back home from a family vacation or congratulate them after they just spoke at a high-profile live-streamed event, which they may have shared on social media. Research reveals commonality, which we'll explore in Chapter 4. Commonality relates to the areas of overlap with others that you can use to connect with others and build a foundation of mutual trust and understanding.

Research helps you explain to yourself and to others why you have your sights set on *this* opportunity and *this* person. It proves that you already know a conversation, interaction, or partnership will be worth the effort and energy for all involved.

In fact, research can help you create value before you interact by saving your contact time, framing a conversation through their

Research helps you explain to yourself and to others why you have your sights set on *this* opportunity and *this* person. It proves that you already know a conversation, interaction, or partnership will be worth the effort and energy for all involved.

current career lens, and making them feel appreciated and their experience recognized.

A more connected digital world is a good thing for research

This book is about elevating networking to be more intentional and mutually rewarding, even as traditional face-to-face networking strategies like in-person events, hand-shaking, and coffee shop meetings are becoming less common and increasingly virtual. The remote meetings and interviews that most would see as restrictions when it comes to professional relationships and job searches are, in fact, a huge opportunity.

For those of us looking to connect more thoughtfully with others about career opportunities, our new level of online connectedness means that there's more research to discover or uncover about contacts in our network.

With more business taking place virtually, less commuter time has translated into more computer time. (And smartphone time too, of course, but the sentence was cuter that way). Due to COVID-19, at-home computer data usage increased by 15 percent, and phone data usage increased 53 percent in March 2020 compared to the previous March.[2] We're building our careers in a primarily digital landscape. If you're a recent or soon-to-be college graduate—a *career builder*—you may be starting your career in this environment. You may even report for your first day of work from home, like I did several years ago for a remote position! It's become imperative to

The remote meetings and interviews that most would see as restrictions when it comes to professional relationships and job searches are, in fact, a huge opportunity.

more prominently represent our personal brands and resumes online. To get noticed, remain relevant, and seek and attract employment and career opportunities, we're sharing more about ourselves in public online spaces like social media and blogs. (Just be smart about using the privacy settings that best suit you, and think about the nature of the content you share in public digital spaces, because future employers will be looking.) And more information is available than ever before about our networks of existing and potential professional contacts. This helps you—or anyone in your network—conduct research and prepare to connect. And, when you're spending more time online, use that time to your advantage to prepare to connect and build quality, positive career relationships.

KNOW MY TOPIC AND MY CONTACT: OPENING THE DOOR TO THIS STEP

Step 1: *Know My Topic and My Contact* is about answers. It's about filling in gaps you may have in your mind about your own pursuits to gain clarity and set direction. And it's about answering questions your contacts may have about you, making it easier for them to connect and bring focus to your collaboration. Conducting appropriate research on career opportunities and contacts helps you and those contacts feel more confident in the relationships you're pursuing.

This step is divided into two elements that you'll use to prepare to connect:

THE KNOCK METHOD
Five steps to open doors and build relationships that matter

High-quality relationship: A mutually beneficial collaboration where both parties contribute and the outcome is stronger

Know my topic, my contact, and specifics up front. Prepare to connect.	**Research/Specifics**
Not about me. Focus on my contacts, us, and our mutual impact.	**Other-Centeredness/ Impact**
Own it. Be personal and authentic; invest in the relationship and the cause up front.	**Authenticity/ Investment**
Commonality. Build trust to open the door.	**Commonality**
Keep giving. Help others and practice generosity and gratitude.	**Generosity/ Gratitude**

1. **Research.** This is about gathering details and information about your contact and your topic so that your interactions with others are well informed. *Research works as a filter.*

2. **Specifics.** The goal of your research is to uncover specific details that you can use to demonstrate that you've done the work up front, to show that you value your contact, and to set direction for a conversation about a topic. You also can reveal details about yourself and have answers to potential questions ready prior to meeting with a contact. *Specifics work as a convincer.*

Research works as a filter.
Specifics work as a convincer.

Through research, you uncover the specifics that can help you prepare to connect more thoughtfully and productively, allowing you to—

1. **Know your topic.** This includes what you're meeting about, your area of interest, and your profession. Your proficiency and knowledge about the topic helps you relate to your contact and exhibit credibility. Be prepared regarding what *you* bring to the relationship: knowledge, experience, and perspective.

2. **Know your contact.** This includes who you're meeting with and the specifics that would make connecting with them relevant to you both. Be prepared regarding what *your contact* brings to the relationship: their knowledge, experience, and perspective.

For example, Jeff Aeder and Jennifer Levine in the Wolcott College Prep story in the earlier chapter, "A New Way to Knock," researched their topic—private schools with specialized learning—and uncovered specifics about tuition, enrollment, and financing so they were better equipped when meeting with prospective donors who had questions about where their money was going. They also got to know their contacts—prospective donors—on an individual level, learning specifics like the likelihood of a donor's child needing the school in the future, and even their donors' favorite sports.

KNOW YOUR TOPIC

This part of Step 1 boils down to: know your stuff. Anticipate the other person's questions to save time and demonstrate that you're worthy of their trust and time. Knowing your topic or area of interest reduces uncertainty for your contact and boosts your own confidence. If you're preparing for a job screening call, for example, anticipate the questions that will come up, and prepare answers to make the interview more effective for everyone. You'll want to know about the job description, comparable salary ranges in the industry, the latest tools and technologies, the company's latest news and what interests you about working there, and how your skill set can contribute to the company's need to hire for this role, all answers to likely questions that will come up. When you don't gather details ahead of time, an interaction can end prematurely or become a much longer string of interactions, resulting in a poor experience for you and the hiring team and inhibiting your career growth.

As I described in my story about Erica Kuhl's pitch to her CMO, she knew her topic: building a community to continue the impact of customer training. She proved the value of her concept with specifics like data for a data-driven leader. She used his favorite tool for presentations, gathered leadership feedback, and had answers to his questions, all before meeting with him, and it paid off.

In the story of MassMutual financial advisor Rick Otis, he knew reaching out to a competitor about pricing for his client's scenario would help him understand if he had the best policy price, as well as give him options to present to his client so he could make an informed decision.

Knowing the ins and outs of the topics you're connecting on with others is an optimal way to show up when building high-quality, positive career relationships. The outcome is progress, productivity, and a mutually beneficial relationship that keeps on giving beyond a single interaction.

KNOW YOUR CONTACT

It's not enough to research topics. Research people, too, before you connect. This isn't about stalkerish behavior where we know someone's every move and violate their privacy. It's about maximizing the tools we have available to learn about people we're connected with in a professional capacity or people we'd like to connect with as we develop our careers. Whether you heard about a particular person from a mutual contact, from the news,

> **Researching your contact is about knowing *about* them before you *know* them.**

from a blog post you read, or from following their personal brand on social media, you can use that public information to connect more thoughtfully. Researching your contact is about knowing *about* them before you *know* them.

I try to arrive early to meet some of the attendees when I teach or speak in front of an audience, or I ask someone where they're calling from before a professional video call starts if I'm one of the first attendees. This helps me get a sense of who is in the room, their level of experience, and what brought them to the event so that I can tailor my speaking points to meet them where they are. I want to know who is in my audience, the individual people who make up the audience.

When it comes to speaking engagements with medium- to large-sized audiences where I may not have the opportunity to get to know each individual, I think of my role as speaking *with* an audience rather than speaking *to* an audience. I often prepare presentation slides but make it known before I start that we can scrap them and simply dive into audience questions if they prefer. Why? Because while they attended to learn about a topic, I often don't have context about how they might apply the topic in their life or career before I walk into the room. I want to ensure the time is valuable for the attendees and myself as the presenter, so the more information I can gather up front about them, the more I can ensure I'm "speaking their language" and sharing relevant information. It also gives them a level of trust at the beginning of the session that the time and attention they're giving to me will be worth it.

> **PRO TIP:** Another way to ensure value for attendees as a speaker is to research the organization you're speaking with. You can post a question or poll on social media in advance of the event, or encourage organizers to send a survey to attendees in advance to get a sense of their expectations, what they're looking to get out of the event, or the most popular questions they're looking to get answered.

RESEARCH

As I stated earlier, research works as a filter. It helps you invest time in relationships that you know—in advance—are likely to have value for both you and your contact. It helps you answer this key question for yourself and for your contact: Should I spend time and effort on this?

You see, go-getter, you may think you're ready to pursue that job because you're excited about it or you're eager to meet with that person because they came highly recommended for a particular opportunity. Take it from me, when I see an exciting opportunity, my first instinct is to jump on it.

Take a quick breath before acting on your excitement.

If you haven't conducted sufficient research, your meeting may end early because you have to go back to get key information. Or you could miss the mark, having set up a meeting with someone who isn't the best fit for the opportunity, resulting in lost time and effort for both of you. Or you may reach out to people who don't respond and feel like you're not making any progress. If you send the same, or slightly edited, messages to a list of prospects or potential employers without doing research to personalize them and present what you've learned in a relevant way, you're unlikely to get a favorable response. Either you haven't sufficiently prepared by getting to know more about the people you're reaching out to, or they weren't the right ones to reach out to in the first place. Spending your time up front on research actually saves time later for you and the other person. By using research as a filter, you can be confident that you're spending time on opportunities with real potential from the get-go.

When your research is successful, you can validate that you're reaching out to the right person by saying, "I know we'll have a lot to talk about because X." You'll be more confident, too, and have fewer doubts about reaching out to senior executives and industry leaders.

Spending your time up front on research actually saves time later for you and the other person.

For example, let's say you work on websites that help retail brands sell their products online. You want to reach out to a retail expert who just wrote an inspiring article in an industry publication because you're looking for ideas and feedback on a new project. You've kept up to date with industry publications and read the expert's career background on LinkedIn to validate that time with her would be valuable to you both, so you decide to send her the following message:

"Hi [Name], I recently came across your article on digital retail trends in X publication. I was particularly inspired by your thoughts on Y because Z. I have a feeling we'll have a lot to talk

about regarding where the mobile retail industry is headed because of my experience building mobile retail apps and your successful career advising the digital retail industry."

This example demonstrates that you did research about your contact's career and uncovered specifics (the article she wrote, the publication name, and the industry—mobile and digital retail) to prove that spending time together would be valuable for both of you. You showed that you knew your topic, in this case the industry because of your professional experience, and knew your contact through your gained knowledge about her professional background and recent article.

Here's how I use research in my career development:

Front-load research to save time and create a more productive interaction later

For career relationship interactions I'm preparing for, I spend time determining who to reach out to and when and how to reach out to them most effectively. Several years ago when I was between jobs, I spent 90 percent of my time preparing and applying for jobs, and only 10 percent actually in interviews and on calls with potential employers and following up afterward. (See Figure 1.1.)

Here's the breakdown:

- **70 percent on research, preparing to connect, and applying for jobs.** I spent this time researching jobs and companies that might be a fit, exploring possible role titles I might pursue, and finding, connecting, or reconnecting with people who could connect me to these opportunities.

- **20 percent on personal branding.** I spent this time polishing and customizing my resume and cover letters for individual opportunities and companies that—based on my research about the company and the role, and connecting with people who worked there—I felt might be a fit and worth pursuing.

- **10 percent on interviews, calls, and follow-up.** I spent this time interviewing and following up with thank-yous and new conversations resulting from my initial interactions.

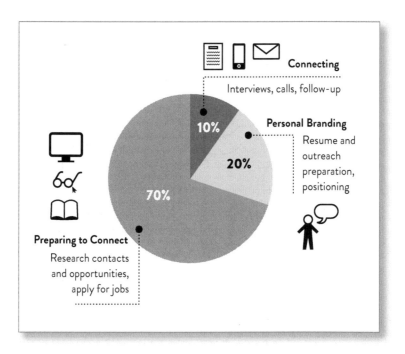

Figure 1.1—Breakdown of time spent before, during, after an interaction with a career contact.

In fact, I kept a spreadsheet of about thirty job opportunities over the course of four months. My research goal was to try to make sure I had one of the following for every opportunity I pursued (research helped me focus on the ones that seemed like the best fit):

- Know a contact at the company I was applying to

- Find a way to connect with someone who worked at that company or in that kind of role

- Reconnect with someone in my network who had a connection to that company

After I connected with someone, I kept notes on how the conversation went, if there were follow-up steps or interviews, and the dates of each conversation. This helped me organize my research, log specifics to track my progress with each opportunity, and prepare for future meetings or second or third interviews in case I needed to reference previous steps in the job search process.

Research was a critical step in my job search for learning about companies. Through research, I found and connected with individuals at the companies I was pursuing employment with, including people on the hiring team that I might work with if I was offered the job, as well as people I knew who could connect me to them. This research also included informational interviews, where I could get a sense of the "day in the life" of someone in the role I was pursuing and understand possible career paths stemming from a similar opportunity. I also asked those I connected with for recommendations of other people I could connect with about the topic and if they'd be willing to make an introduction, thus keeping the door open and unlocking additional opportunities during my career discovery.

Since research serves as a filter, preparing to connect with employers helped me weed out opportunities that would not be worth the time to pursue. It helped me gather specifics I could use in interviews that piqued my interest like company culture, upcoming conferences, recent news, company acquisitions, and even stock prices and trends.

Spend time to get to know my contacts

As I previously mentioned, I meet with audience attendees in advance of a class or speaking engagement to get to know them on a personal level and tailor the presentation to their specific needs to make it a valuable use of their time. When I meet with professional contacts, whether in a mentoring capacity or simply to share ideas, I listen to them and pick up on their personal interests, which I can ask for updates on in later conversations, and begin to build more of a human interaction, rather than a transactional one that only takes place when I'm in need of some career advice or help.

Think through the details and plans up front to present my topic in a more productive way

When I decided I wanted to write a book, I prepared a book proposal for prospective publishers. This proposal included details like target audience and its size, competitive analysis of similar books to prove there's a market for the topic, a marketing plan, a chapter outline with detailed summaries, and sample chapters. This proposal served as my own list of frequently asked questions (FAQ) so publishers could get to know the details of my book concept and also see the work I put into developing the concept and gauge potential for book sales. The same goes for career conversations. Based on the topic you're meeting about, have your own FAQs in your back pocket so that you're prepared when questions arise. You'll be able to show you've done your work and that you're ready for whatever comes from the interaction. If others feel you're willing to put effort into a relationship, they may be more inclined to give to it too.

SPECIFICS

If research works as a filter, then the specifics work as a convincer. Specifics help your contact find something to latch onto that feels relevant to them and paint a clearer picture about what you can both bring to the table. Uncovering specifics from the research on your topic and your contact, and about yourself, helps answer questions before they're asked, convincing your contact that you're relevant to them and worth investing time with.

Let's continue with the digital retail example earlier in this chapter. Based on the research you did, you've highlighted the specifics about your industry and your topic that you know are relevant to your contact. You'll also want to share specifics about yourself and the value you and your contact can bring to each other. In this way, you can reduce any doubts your contact may have and ensure they're investing in a relationship that your research proves will be worth it. In your email to the retail expert, rather than simply providing a general introduction and asking for her time, you'll want to include a bit more about who you are and why you're reaching out. By showcasing your research and revealing specifics about the topic and yourself in your initial message, you'll answer any questions she might have, like "Who is this person? How did they find me? Why are they reaching out? If we met, what would we talk about? Will this be worth my time?" In that same message, when you introduce yourself, you might say something like:

"I'm [Name], a retail website designer for athletic wear brands out of Chicago. I'm working on some new website features like touch screen technology and biometrics to make retail more fun, human-centric, and automated. In your article, you mentioned contactless shopping, and I'm curious about your thoughts on some of the technology I'm looking to use."

Without specifics, it's hard to convince someone to give you time for an interaction. It's just like when you interview for a job and the hiring manager asks, "Why are you interested in this company?" If the answer is, "I know it's a great company," the vague, general response raises questions about whether you've done your research and have a clear idea of direction. It might introduce doubt and make it difficult to convince someone that 1) you have researched and narrowed in on specific types of opportunities that your skill set is a fit for and 2) you would contribute in the role. Not doing research makes it difficult for others to help you along your career path because if you're unsure of your own direction, they certainly won't know where to focus their help. Of course, having casual and spontaneous conversations with career contacts can help you set direction, but if and when you can prepare in advance and have specifics at the ready, they can help focus a planned conversation.

Not doing research makes it difficult for others to help you along your career path because if you're unsure of your own direction, they certainly won't know where to focus their help.

Here's another example. Suppose someone reaches out to you and says:

"Hi. Your friend Josh said I should reach out to you. I'm a recent college grad looking for my first job. Could we meet for coffee?"

You probably have so many questions about what she studied, how she knows Josh, what kind of job she's looking for, if she knows what kind of job she's looking for, where she lives, when and where you might consider meeting, and so on.

But, if she provided specifics about herself and even about scheduling a meeting, she might write something like this:

"Hi X, our mutual friend Josh, my family's neighbor, suggested I reach out and thought we'd have an interesting conversation about careers in finance. I just graduated from the University of Texas with a finance degree and am pursuing an analyst job with local, medium-sized firms in Austin like yours. My strengths are in building investment models, and I have a forward-thinking mentality. I'm curious about how finance has changed from your perspective since you began your career when Josh did. Would you be open to a 15–30 minute casual career conversation one morning this week between 8 a.m. and 10 a.m. CST?"

Specifics provide you with a clearer picture of who the student is and answers more of your questions up front, making it easy and compelling to respond, and convincing you that meeting with this graduate would be a productive conversation.

Get specific, but not too specific, which can limit your relationship potential. This balance is important. Specifics are about providing helpful details to build a connection with your contacts. However, if you get so specific that you jump out of the gate with a one-sided ask and don't leave much room for getting to know each other, or for catching up if it's with an existing contact, you may be getting into transactional relationship territory that doesn't feel so good and isn't mutually beneficial.

Jessica Malkin, former CEO of Chicago Ideas, says practicing connectivity and relationship building for a bigger purpose doesn't come easily to everyone; it often feels foreign, and they don't know where to begin. She believes a lot of people today are unfamiliar with, and often not receptive to, serendipitous connection, or random conversation in person or on the phone.

It's not in their comfort zone, so they wait until the day they need something.

She advised: "If you're going to be good at building personal relationships, you can't just text [behind screens], you need to converse with people live and have serendipitous conversations where you go down a rabbit hole—that's more natural and it will take you outside of the bounds of what you know you want to talk about."

One way to find the right balance between providing specifics and leaving the door open to discover ways to collaborate in the long term is to use facts. You might say this:

"I noticed you've been with a company for ten years. You're a few years ahead of me on this career path. Maybe you could shed some light on where you see the industry going."

With this approach, you can highlight specifics you've heard, seen, read, or watched about them in your research, but also provide them with an opportunity to either correct what you've said or build on it.

Use specifics when they can help you paint a clearer picture about why you're reaching out, or have them in your mind (or your notes) and use them if the conversation needs them. But take the time to listen, and leave some room to discover or rediscover each other and have some natural conversation. That's the beauty of building positive, high-quality, long-lasting career relationships—they go beyond one interaction and are not limited to a specific need; they keep giving on both sides and have lasting potential to make a bigger impact.

RESEARCH AND TIMING GO TOGETHER

Consider timing when reaching out to a contact. Research can uncover details about what a person or company has going on, so that when you reach out or meet, you're sensitive to those things or their schedule. For example, when reaching out to business leaders for interviews to include in this book, I reviewed their recent social media posts to get a snapshot of their latest endeavors. Then I'd mention a recent event they participated in, an article they wrote, or a trip they just took.

Once, I sent a message to a conference speaker while I was in the audience and he was on stage because I thought his story would be inspiring for the book. He noticed it as soon as he got off the stage, responded, and we set up a time to meet up later during his trip (I was amazed at his generosity—hello, Chapter 5). Later, when I was preparing to reach out to this nonprofit leader to ask him to review the book chapter with his story in it, I checked his LinkedIn updates because I knew that he posts there often and it was a busy time for his organization. I noticed his company had a Facebook Live event taking place at that very moment—I'm not even kidding! I joined the livestream in time to hear his concluding thoughts. When I sent him the email, I let him know I joined the online event that day and mentioned something he said that inspired me, to show that I value him beyond the chapter review. Note that this extra effort to connect more thoughtfully only took a few minutes, but it made a significant difference because I was connecting on a human level, not just for an outcome.

Take cues from your research that will help make career conversations relevant to your contact. This is just like keeping up with friends and asking about their recent life updates. When you send an email or get together, you'll mention things they had going on and ask about them. To spark and keep relationships going, spend some time to familiarize or reorient yourself to someone's life and career happenings, before connecting, to demonstrate your interest in them and feed conversation topics. Consider timing, including what's going on in current events and in a contact's life, when you connect with others. If you're prepared, and when, based on research, you uncover details and specifics, you can have a more vivid and dynamic interaction. Of course, not everything can be revealed through research because so much of our lives is not shared publicly or in the limelight. That's why the human element of connecting with others—asking how someone is doing before starting a call or a meeting—is important. I can't tell you how many times I have planned to have specific conversations with my managers at work, when I realized they were having a bad day or had differing priorities from my own, and I adjusted our agenda on the fly, simply taking time to listen and respond, setting my own direction aside. And, when I was just starting out in my career, my upcoming performance review meetings were the most important thing I had on my mind, and my managers, who were juggling a big team and lots of priorities, rescheduled, which frustrated me. Shifting priorities when people come together to connect is natural and par for the course. Timing when you connect with others is important, so preparing *when* to connect should also be intentional.

If you're not sure what to put into a message or what to say in a conversation with a contact, you may not have done sufficient research. That's when you know it's not an optimal time to meet or maximize your time together.

Here's a tool to help you determine if you're ready to reach out or meet with a contact.

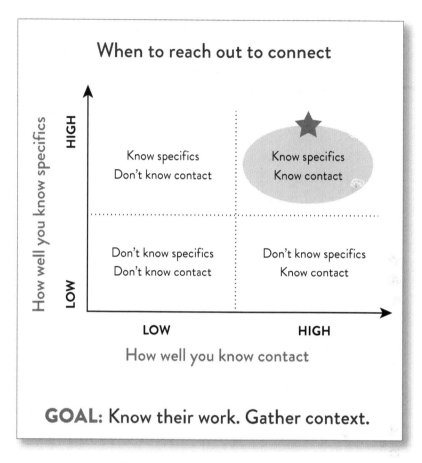

Figure 1.2 (Resource #3 in the Appendix)

When you do the research and gather specifics to know your topic and your contact, you'll have answers to their questions and your own, and have confidence that you're ready for a productive conversation. Doesn't being prepared feel good?

Email Example Spotlight

The following email is an edited version of the one I sent to a colleague, Adam H., when I was looking for a mentor. He has now been my mentor for three years. Notice how I highlight specifics from my research and about myself to make the message relevant to my contact throughout, but I also leave the conversation open to get to know each other rather than ask for a mentor right off the bat.

January 2017

Hi Adam,

My name is Rebecca Otis and I am a strategic marketing consultant . . . also on the Customer Success Group team out of Chicago, working with [Client A], [Client B], and [Client C]. We haven't had the pleasure of meeting yet, but I was researching **employees at our company on LinkedIn who also teach at the university level [Commonality, Research]** (which I am currently pursuing to supplement my full-time role).

I came across your profile and noticed **you not only teach at [X university] (awesome!), [Research, Specifics, Other Centeredness]** but we have several **mutual contacts including [Person A] at [X company] and [Person B]. [Commonality]** We appear to have a **shared interest in tracking marketing trends, leading organizations toward those trends, and public speaking about them! [Commonality, Research, Specifics]** I blog and teach, so all in all, it appears we might have some interesting ways to learn from each other.

I'm curious if you have become familiar with our internal mentoring program? I am excited that our leadership is encouraging career nurturing opportunities. While the thought crossed my mind to ask if you might have a few moments to spare on a regular basis as my mentor, I like to connect *first—and believe in building mutually beneficial relationships—before jumping into such an ask!*

*Would you be interested in connecting on a quick phone call? At a minimum, I'd love to share perspectives from our respective teams and learn more about **your marketing team**. **[Other-Centeredness]** What do you think?*

I look forward to hearing from you, Adam.

HOW DO YOU DO IT?

Here's how to connect with others by using research and specifics as a filter and a convincer and bringing them to the forefront in interactions to prove up-front effort and credibility.

Work your way down

Start off with the most widely available resources, and work your way down to the most focused, direct resources. (See Figure 1.3.) Let's say you're looking to connect with three startup founders at tech companies in your city of Denver to research how to get started with your own tech startup and find potential partners. You may start broadly by searching Google for "top Denver tech startups" to see who comes up in the news, then visit their websites to see if their products may be relevant, and search their "About Us" page to read up on their founders. Now, you've made a list of up to ten founders who look like they may have relevant experience and products that your product may be able to integrate with in the future. You look up all ten on social media and find five that have active accounts with helpful startup-related posts. You follow them to keep up with their latest news. After following them for a week or two, you find three for which sharing ideas would be mutually productive. You go to LinkedIn, look them up, and notice you have mutual contacts with two of them. You reach out to your mutual contacts to reconnect and ask if they'd be willing to connect you with the two startup founders, sharing specifics of what you're looking to connect about. You invite the third founder to connect on LinkedIn, including a message that mentions their startup news from social media and that you're looking to connect to share ideas because you're new to the tech startup world in Denver and are about to launch a product. If only a couple respond or you feel you have much more to learn, you can always repeat this exercise with a new set of ten individuals or companies or go back to your list of ten prospects to see if there are valuable ways to connect with the remaining seven.

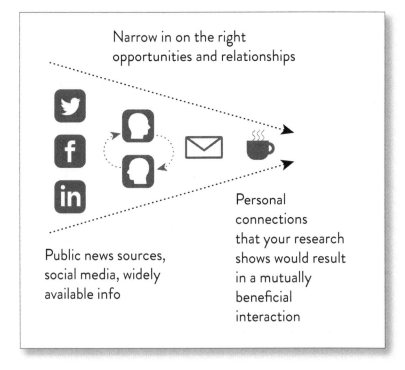

Figure 1.3—Research as a filter: How to narrow in on connections from broad, public information sources to the most direct to ensure time spent with the most valuable interactions.

Put yourself in their shoes

Put yourself in the shoes of your contact, and answer their questions before they ask them. Research will be your filter for determining what you're pursuing and why. What might your contact want to know about you or your goals?

For example, if you're applying for a job, you'll want to have answers to the following questions ready:

- **Why are you applying to this role and this company?** This is likely the first and most important question that will come up as you pursue a new job. If you've done your research, you'll be able to provide memorable specifics about how the role relates to your professional experience and what most interests you about the company. You will use this information in your cover letter and in interviews, and it will differentiate you from other candidates.

- **What is the average salary for similar jobs?** Prospective employers may want to know your salary expectations. Research can help you define them. This can also help you confirm an opportunity is in line with your level of experience and what you're truly looking for.

- **What is the typical career path, and what are growth opportunities for someone currently in this role?** As part of your research, you may want to talk to someone in that role at the company to shed some light. Prospective employers may ask you what your career goals are and where you see yourself in three to five years, and this knowledge can help you prepare that answer.

Present knowledge from your research

When the time is right, you can present the key knowledge from your research. If you're conversing with a prospective donor to your nonprofit, it can be helpful to have statistics available to share if you're asked about the impact your organization makes and where the dollars go. You may not need to share this information at the beginning of your conversation. But if you're meeting with someone about a grant, sharing the size and impact of your organization up front may give them context for the level of funding that might be appropriate. Do your research to be prepared, and then share it when it's appropriate, based on the situation. You don't have to share everything all at once, and some of it you may use simply to help you prepare more thoughtfully, rather than during your interaction with others.

For Rick Otis, the financial advisor who helped Mr. K get an insurance policy, research is crucial. Preparation makes all the difference for trust, efficiency (saving people time weighing information and options), and positive outcomes (helping more people with financial security).

"I always show up with an idea so people understand what I do or information that will benefit them so they know I'm prepared," Rick said. Many people in his profession feel they need to interview prospects or clients first, then bring them ideas. But as Rick said, "I never know if I'll get a second chance, so I'll bring ideas the first time we meet." For example, he does research and shows stats such as how other people with his prospect's profile manage their finances. According to Rick, "Ninety-nine percent of the time, people will buy that research-backed concept. If I find out there are holes in people's plans that need to get fixed right away, I try to

> **"I never know if I'll get a second chance, so I'll bring ideas the first time we meet."**
>
> —Rick Otis

fill them. I don't wait. I feel it's unethical to not fill that void right away." He prepares so he can have solutions, no matter the challenge that arises.

Rick also says, "I never go to a new appointment without a concept." This is similar to how I came to the product team at my company with an inventory of resources to review. I prepared to connect and brought something for the team to react to.

How does Rick prepare to go into a meeting with someone new? When is the right time to meet with someone? "I generally won't go into a meeting unless I know something about them," he said. Rick knows about his contact before he *knows* them.

> ## "I generally won't go into a meeting unless I know something about them."
>
> —Rick Otis

He also creates opportunity out of existing client relationships. "I'm proactive and I create strategies for people [that] they didn't even ask for because they don't know it exists," he said. "I know their situation because of ongoing, mutually beneficial relationships and trust, and I can provide an idea that I think is good for them to consider." His preparation makes meetings more productive and helpful for his clients.

KNOW MY TOPIC AND MY CONTACT: KEY TIPS TO APPLY THIS STEP

- **Before any meeting, think of two to five questions.** Base them on what you know about your contact to guide your conversation. Do not go to any meeting without some topics or questions in mind. Take a couple of minutes to do a quick search on LinkedIn, ask a mutual contact about the person you'll be meeting with, or search your internal company organization chart in advance. Think of these questions or topics in the car on the way to the meeting, or when you have ten minutes before joining the call, for example. Meet an audience before speaking with or teaching them to tailor your message to be relevant to them.

- **Know specifics up front, and present them when the time is right.** If you know your contact likes running and your meeting is on a Monday, start off by asking if they got a run in over the weekend. Or maybe you know they are involved in a children's organization, which might come up when you talk about their company's involvement in the local community.

- **Create your own list of frequently asked questions (FAQs).** Anticipate what questions will come up by putting yourself in your contact's shoes. Prepare answers for those questions.

2

NOT ABOUT ME

Demonstrate other-centeredness and highlight impact—it's about my contact, others, and "us"

I wrote this book for you, my readers, and for my community—past, present, and future. I believe in bringing the power of what we can do together to the surface, sharing inspiring stories that exemplify this notion of looking outward and dedicating work to the impact we can make, rather than how it helps us as individuals. This outward-looking approach and mentality will have a ripple effect. It will strengthen our collective network, uncover new partnerships, and shorten the distance between individuals and teams so that we can progress further together.

This chapter covers the cornerstone step in The Knock Method, Step 2: *Not About*

All other steps are centered around what this step is about: the approach of shifting focus from ourselves to others, and what we can achieve when we partner with others as we build long-lasting relationships in our careers.

Me. All other steps are centered around what this step is about: the approach of shifting focus from ourselves to others, and what we can achieve when we partner with others as we build long-lasting relationships in our careers. Want an example? Here's a story that demonstrates the significant outcomes that come from shifting our perspective and behavior from focusing on our own benefit, to focusing on mutually beneficial relationships.

FROM COLD CALL TO COLD SHOULDER

In 2009, Adam Lowy was in his twenties and just getting started in his career, but he knew he had an in. His father, cofounder of Lowy's Moving Service, was affiliated with Wheaton World Wide Moving, a moving company with a vast network of 250 moving agents and partners covering 95 percent of the United States. So Adam was sure he could get the then president of Wheaton, Dave, to help with his idea to move food to the hungry.

Adam's new concept—Move for Hunger[1]—would use space in large moving trucks already on the road to carry excess nonperishable food items from people's homes to local food banks, reducing waste while helping those in need. He asked Dave for $100,000.

It backfired. Dave not only said no, but he asked Wheaton to sever all ties with Adam and his father's company.

Adam realized that his request had come off as unsubstantiated and aggressive. It did not accurately present the value that Wheaton would bring to the partnership or the impact Wheaton's contribution would make in communities nationwide. In other words, it was a one-sided, short-term ask without a lot of explanation—not to mention, a big one. He went from cold call to cold shoulder.

How could he recover? Adam called his primary contact, a

marketing lead at Wheaton, and said, "I really messed this up. What can I do to fix it? I know many of your agents really like the concept." He apologized to his contact, owned up to his error, and immediately highlighted the impact and the value that the concept was already making, not for his charity, but for *Wheaton*. The shift from focusing on his own needs to what the partnership could accomplish for Wheaton's agents and in the fight against hunger was crucial.

The new, more humble, and other-centered approach paid off. Wheaton's marketing lead persuaded Dave to get back in touch with Adam, and so Dave did, suggesting that they meet in person during an upcoming trip to the East Coast. A few weeks later, Adam, his father, and his uncle sat down to meet with Dave. Adam apologized and presented a new approach focused on the impact of the program for Wheaton. He then explained how he had calculated the dollar amount he asked for.

This conversation enabled Dave to better understand the concept and the impact it could make to address hunger in communities nationwide, as well as the value for Wheaton. Although Adam tried to get him on board by offering to give Wheaton the PR value of being an exclusive partner, Dave was already thinking more expansively. Dave felt this initiative was bigger than one moving company and that Wheaton and Move for Hunger should work together to mobilize the entire industry. Adam's assumption about what Dave would value—exclusivity—was off, which became clear only when they sat down to talk, listened to each other, shared ideas, and found ways to help each other. That worked far better than jumping out of the gate with that hefty initial ask based on an inaccurate assumption.

In the end, Wheaton made a $10,000 donation, and Dave served on the board of Move for Hunger for several years. During this time, Dave made introductions to other leaders in the moving industry, giving Move for Hunger instant legitimacy and even more fuel for the organization's launch than $100,000, Adam's initial donation request, possibly could have.

"He taught me it's not just about the money," Adam reflected. "Especially in the early stage, some things are significantly more valuable than money, like connections and credibility, and having leaders in your corner who really understand the impact you can make together.

"It's not always about what you can get, but also about what you can give," he explained to me. "[A partnership] should always be two-way, both providing value."

Adam had learned that he needed more than financial investment to sustain the organization; he needed a network of partners who believed in the cause and could expand the organization's reach.

"Especially in the early stage, some things are significantly more valuable than money, like connections and credibility, and having leaders in your corner who really understand the impact you can make together."

—Adam Lowy

Wheaton's partnership was crucial to the growth of Move for Hunger, which started a pilot program with eight moving companies that Wheaton had recruited. This gave the charity national reach, with moving partners in many states.

Then Adam set his sights higher. To prepare for a booth at a conference of two hundred moving companies hosted by Wheaton, Adam created customized letters for attendees from each company, featuring statistics about hunger in the company's local market. He put the letters in folders, each labeled with an attendee's name, and then found each attendee at the conference and delivered the folders in person. Again, Adam made a personalized pitch about each company as a future partner, highlighted hunger needs in their individual markets, and emphasized the potential impact that joining the cause could make in *their* communities.

Move for Hunger's member participation grew from one mover to six hundred in just five years, growth that was accomplished without direct mail, advertising dollars, or cold calling (except that first presumptuous call).

Move for Hunger saw immediate success at a time when the economy was recovering from a recession and companies had been cutting charitable ties to save money. How? The charity built a model that would be easy to implement and could be integrated into each company's business. Move for Hunger provided boxes and materials to make transporting the food easy, so it could become part of a moving company's business model.

Through 2019, Adam was on the road fifteen weeks a year to shake the hands of Move for Hunger partners, to let them know they were appreciated and to recognize them for what they were doing for the cause. He continues to showcase the collective impact for new partners and why they should think about joining.

Move for Hunger asks partners to commit to transporting three hundred pounds of food, or ten boxes, to local food banks. It mobilizes its corporate partners to encourage agents to participate. To keep partnerships alive and the industry's impact top of mind, Move for Hunger recognizes the most impactful mover of the year at the American Moving & Storage Association conference.

As I write this, Move for Hunger has delivered more than seventeen million pounds of food to food banks and provided fourteen million meals to individuals facing hunger across the country since its inception. The first year it raised more than $1 million was 2019, and the charity accomplished that with a staff of just thirteen. They manage one thousand movers, fifteen hundred property management partners, and fifteen hundred food drives, which resulted in delivering 2.6 million pounds of food in 2019.

HOW ADAM KNOCKS

What contributed to Move for Hunger's success? After the rejection of his cold call, Adam shifted his focus away from how others could help him and toward the value for his potential partners' communities and individuals facing hunger, and their collective impact. It wasn't about what *he* could accomplish, it was about what Wheaton and other partners, together with Move for Hunger, could achieve to fight national hunger.

Now, let's dive into the meaning of this step in The Knock Method.

THE KNOCK METHOD STEP 2 IN ACTION

Not about me (Other-Centeredness)	Listened and learned to shift his approach to focusing on what investing in Move for Hunger would do for Wheaton.
Not about me (Impact)	Positioned the value for potential partners considering joining the Move for Hunger network. Focused on the impact the Move for Hunger network could make together to address hunger nationwide rather than the importance to Adam.

NOT ABOUT ME: THIS STEP IN CONTEXT

This step is the reason why The Knock Method came to be. In my own career experiences as a blogger and working in the SEO industry, and when I felt my consulting expertise was undervalued,

I found a lack of rich partnerships in the business environment around me, an environment saturated with self-serving attitudes and business practices that took a toll on professional relationships, rather than enriching them.

I wondered, "What caused this behavior?" I dove into some research for some answers, and here is what I found.

Before you can realistically think about focusing on others, it's important to consider your own sense of self in relation to others. For example, in the career context, do you focus more on the greater good of a company, an industry, or the economy through your work or on boosting your personal brand and how others in your network perceive you? There's no wrong answer here, unless you take either perspective to the extreme (for example, by failing to speak up for yourself or by focusing only on yourself). You likely value a balance between the two approaches.

When thinking about how you see yourself in work and social relationships, consider this view as more of a spectrum where individuals, organizations, cultures, societies, and even generations vary in their focus-on-others to focus-on-self ratio.

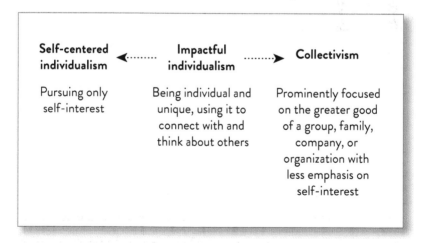

Figure 2.1—Find the balance between having
a sense of self and being other-centered.

To explain what I mean by this, let's explore two social science theories: collectivism and individualism. (See Figure 2.1.)

Collectivism is a principle where people put group goals and long-term relationships above personal goals and self-interest. Here's the positive side of collectivism: It creates an outward-looking perspective, one where your efforts are part of something greater. The drawbacks are that if you only identify with the groups you are a part of and don't think about what unique skills and experience you bring to the table, you might feel lost, unmotivated, and unfulfilled. Even for those of us who are introverts, we all want to be seen for who we are and not get lost in the crowd.

Individualism is a social psychology term describing a focus on your personal goals, your identity, and how others perceive you.[2] An individualistic society is the opposite of a collectivist one and gives priority to personal goals rather than ones that benefit a community, group, or society as a whole.[3] On the positive side, it elevates your desire to be unique, advocate for yourself, and differentiate yourself from others to succeed. The corporate world actually programs us to take on this mindset to get ahead, and in a fully digital and social world, we now have more tools than ever that enable us to create, own, and amplify our voices.

The downside of individualism is that if you focus only on yourself and your interests, it can manifest into a self-centered attitude with a low regard for helping and partnering with others. Not only is it limiting, it can be isolating, which as you now know, is detrimental to your health too.

In an effort to get an education, get a job, then get the next job and rise to the next level, or build a company, then grow the company, then seek to get said company acquired—whether for drive, passion, compensation, wealth, fame, followers, or simply the chase—we may find ourselves hustling in the hamster wheel.

This pursuit happens at the expense of deep, quality, long-lasting relationships, and at the expense of valuing others. Along the way, we may find we have overcompensated by trying to be so individualistic that we failed to see the positive impact we could make on and with others.

We're in the thick of the influencer movement, with the ability to create, share, and celebrate our personal brands using social media with devices constantly at our fingertips. When we see those who focus only on themselves in these public spaces, this creates a perception that the millennial generation and the generations bookending it are thirsty for attention, and that attention equals self-worth. The more we yearn for personal attention, individuality, and our own voice, the less we are focused on partnerships, togetherness, and others.

Not everyone is extremely individualistic, but those who are have given taking a self-interest a bad reputation. While cultural generalizations about youth and the rise of social media suggest that millennials (those born between 1981 and 1996) are more self-centered and narcissistic (me-me-me mentality) than other generations,[4] academic researchers are still studying this theory[5] and have not proven it true. Instead, psychologists have discovered that while millennials and younger generations do place importance on individualism, it didn't just rise suddenly. Individualism has been rising consistently since the late 1800s, it applies to people of all ages, and it is related to the increase in white-collar jobs, economic status, globalization, and access to education and information.[6]

Think about it. More education, jobs, and financial wealth means people have the means and flexibility to travel, uncover new ideas, move for jobs, change jobs, and even create their own businesses based on their unique ideas.[7]

A lot of good has come from this rise in individualism over the last century—new job types, entrepreneurialism, and a rise in remote work that enables mobility and lifestyle flexibility while maintaining productivity and well-being. Some individualism is healthy and has made our dynamic economy and career landscape full of the opportunities they have today. Plus, an individualistic society like ours has also proven to be altruistic—or giving.[8]

How can it be that, if you're inwardly focused, you can still find a way to think about and help others?

In collectivist societies, people have such close ties with others that they may shut new people or others out. Meanwhile, individualism focuses on having a unique voice and sense of self. If you exhibit and value what I call *impactful individualism*—a degree of individualism that's also focused on your contributions to the greater good—you may be more open to new ideas and the unique characteristics that others bring to an interaction. (See Figure 2.1.) If you have the urge to be unique and original, then you may relate to others who are also carving their own paths, *and* you may be more inclined to help them.

If you exhibit and value what I call impactful individualism—a degree of individualism that's also focused on your contributions to the greater good—you may be more open to new ideas and the unique characteristics that others bring to an interaction.

While it may seem counterintuitive that shifting focus off of ourselves can help us carve our own individual paths to professional and personal success, this book is about just that—approaching relationships with a focus on others. When we do this effectively, we differentiate ourselves from the self-centric world around us.

If you live your life exclusively valuing *self-centered individualism*, this will not work. The current economy, communication style, social media, and influencer craze create a self-centered—rather than an other-centered—tide. If we're not conscious of it, we can get swept up in it.

Examples of this are all around us, and it's easy to fall into the trap of picking up our smartphones one more time to see how many "Likes" our latest post got, then posting again for a quick surge of dopamine and to quench our curiosity. As a millennial who succumbs to this urge now and again (okay, let's be honest, more than just every once in a while), and also one who looked into this matter, rest assured that not everyone who values individualism takes it to the extreme, without regard for others.

Pausing to become aware of this environment where self-interest can take over, and focusing on others and what we can do together before—and when—building relationships, counteract this harmful mindset.

This book is intended to generate self-awareness to counteract our self-involved digital landscape. Simply taking a moment to think about shifting our perspective outward when building relationships, focusing on the value we can bring to others, and maximizing the impact we can make together can make all the difference. And, by now, you're already thinking about it, so you're on the right path.

Simply taking a moment to think about shifting our perspective outward when building relationships, focusing on the value we can bring to others, and maximizing the impact we can make together can make all the difference.

People and companies are taking action to disconnect from the attention economy. For example, REI has its "Opt Outside" holiday campaign[9] in which it closes its stores on Black Friday to encourage people to get out into the world and work on making it a better place. Maybe you've jumped on the bandwagon on the National Day of Unplugging[10] on the first Friday of March so you can spend more time living authentic experiences and connecting with family and friends.

These initiatives counter our tendency to fall into a hyperconnected digital world often saturated with lower quality transactional interactions with others. Individualism can coexist with our innate yearn to give to and help others, and gives us confidence, too.

Simply being aware of how you approach relationships in your career and social spheres, and finding a balance between self-interest and other-centeredness, will contribute to a shift in your community and network. The future is bright for more outward-looking and thoughtful relationship building for mutual benefit in our careers and our lives.

> ## Simply being aware of how you approach relationships in your career and social spheres, and finding a balance between self-interest and other-centeredness, will contribute to a shift in your community and network.

It's reassuring to know that we can be individualistic *and* other-centered. In fact, as you read on, think about how you can bring your unique experiences to professional relationships to make them richer and more fruitful, with a positive impact on others.

That's why taking a "not about me" approach stands out, and why it succeeds in opening the door to productive and positive career relationships.

When it comes to being individualistic and valuing human-kind as a whole, we *can* do both. Let's swing the pendulum back toward the middle of the spectrum (see Figure 2.1) from a self-centered individualistic extreme to the bigger impact we can make together.

Focus on the quality of your human relationships instead of the quantity of interactions. And focus on your combined impact with others, rather than transactional this-for-that interactions in pursuit of your own goals. Slow down to gain awareness about how you present yourself in relation to others, beyond your personal brand, to your contributions to work, to your partnerships with others. You'll make progress as you develop your career through thoughtful relationship building. When you do this, you will stand out from the pack, quench your thirst for individual-ism, and help others simultaneously. Note to my fellow efficiency enthusiasts: You might even accomplish more and have a lasting impact on our communities and our world.

Let's take a look at what the science says about the two con-cepts in Step 2: *Not About Me*: other-centeredness and impact. Why does focusing on others when forging career relationships work, and how can it help you, even in your quest for individual-ity, efficiency, and professional success?

THE KNOCK METHOD
Five steps to open doors and build relationships that matter

High-quality relationship: A mutually beneficial collaboration where both parties contribute and the outcome is stronger

Know my topic, my contact, and specifics up front. Prepare to connect.	**Research/Specifics**
Not about me. Focus on my contacts, us, and our mutual impact.	**Other-Centeredness/ Impact**
Own it. Be personal and authentic; invest in the relationship and the cause up front.	**Authenticity/ Investment**
Commonality. Build trust to open the door.	**Commonality**
Keep giving. Help others and practice generosity and gratitude.	**Generosity/ Gratitude**

NOT ABOUT ME:
OPENING THE DOOR TO THIS STEP

Step 2: *Not About Me* is made up of two elements:

1. **Other-centeredness.** When building professional relationships, focus on others rather than yourself.

2. **Impact.** When building professional relationships, highlight a greater purpose than your individual career endeavors.

Showcase the difference that you and an individual, a group, a company, or a community can make together.

Even as you see successful career relationships developing around you, and in stories like those in this book, you should understand the science of why and how they work. Psychology research helps explain why building relationships in a thoughtful way is important, not only for ourselves, but for those close to us, for our broader communities, and for our world.

Next, we'll explore the concept of other-centeredness and the importance of highlighting impact when interacting with others in career relationships. Both will help you shift focus off of yourself and onto others for a greater collective benefit.

OTHER-CENTEREDNESS

Other-centeredness is a form of prosociality, or acting in ways that benefit others.[11] Helping, sharing, and comforting are other-centered behaviors. We behave in ways that help others in our social lives and even in our careers.[12] While our instinct dating back to early civilization is to keep to and protect ourselves and our clan, thinking of and helping others are also part of our DNA. We can't ignore the fact that humankind does act in the best interest of others and that cooperation is essential.[13] Let's reactivate this innate need at our core to partner with others and apply it to developing our careers.

For example, when a colleague I worked with reached out because his design role had been eliminated due to shifting company priorities, he asked for a LinkedIn recommendation. I happily provided one for his work as he sought a new role. But I could do more to help. I had been in a position previously when my role was at risk of being eliminated during a company acquisition, and I really felt for him. I connected him with two individuals in the same field with a similar design skill set to broaden his network and discuss potential job opportunities. He didn't ask for the connections, but I checked with him and my contacts to make sure they were on board with my making introductions, and they all agreed. I practiced other-centered behavior (although I didn't think of it in this scientific way at the time) simply because I thought my colleague had top-notch talent and I wanted to help him so that he found a new employment opportunity quickly. Connections like this could also help those I'm connecting him with to fill open roles with highly qualified employees. I would hope that if I were in a similar position, my contacts would help me connect with others so I could progress in my job search, even if there were no clear benefit to them at the time other than helping another.

HOW DO YOU DO IT?

Along your career path, when it's time to connect with someone, think about how you can learn about, listen to, and focus on *them*. Of course, it's not *only* about them, or it wouldn't be a relationship.[14] After all, you play a critical part in any relationship that you cultivate. Instead of focusing on what you can get from someone, think about what you can both give to a partnership and a bigger cause. As I mentioned earlier, we can be individualistic and collectivist. It's okay to pursue your career goals *and* focus on others; it's *how* you do it that matters.

Avoid transactional, or this-for-that, strategic, or conditional networking (I'll help you for X or if Y . . .). Why? Otherwise, an interaction might stop at just that—an interaction rather than an ongoing relationship.

Create an experience, rather than an exchange.

It could become transactional and emotionless, and feel more mechanical and less human. Sad, right? It could burn out quickly or the door could close in your face, as it did in Adam Lowy's case when he first reached out to Wheaton World Wide Moving for support for his new nonprofit.

When approached differently, with deliberate preparation and emphasis on your contacts, an interaction could turn into a long-term, mutually beneficial relationship that keeps giving with no strings attached. I'll provide resources at the end of this chapter to put Step 2: *Not About Me* into practice and begin applying it to your career.

You might wonder how I got the interviews in this book. By using The Knock Method, of course! The email examples and stories scattered throughout these chapters reveal the details. But mostly, it had to do with really paying attention to role models, industry

It's okay to pursue your career goals *and* focus on others; it's *how* you do it that matters.

leaders, and successful professionals who clearly demonstrated that they achieved their success through building thoughtful relationships, breeding inclusivity, and creating community. I met some of them serendipitously and followed up intentionally or through mutual connections; with others I took extra time to invest in their work and do research to open the door to a productive conversation for both of us. Then, after researching each individual and learning more about what's important to them—using Step 1: *Know My Topic and My Contact*, I tailored my actions and communications to be about them, making the focus "not about me."

For example, when I interviewed Julie Smolyansky, CEO of Lifeway Foods, whom you'll read about in an upcoming chapter, I had already met her, taken a photo with her at her cookbook signing, and interviewed her for my blog and this book, and we kept the relationship going. I follow her on Instagram. One Friday, several years after the blog interview, while scrolling (don't we all?), I saw her post that she was in Denver, where I live, for a wellness conference. I immediately sent her a direct message and asked how long she'd be in town and offered to take her to lunch so we could catch up. As busy as she is, she still made the time to respond, letting me know her time was limited, but she extended an invitation for me to stop by the conference to see her presentation later that day. I decided to take her up on the offer to reconnect briefly in person since the convention center was just down the street. When I arrived, she had arranged for her assistant to meet me at the entrance with a volunteer badge! (What a generous offer!) Within an hour and a half, I was listening to her share her wellness mindset on stage. When we caught up afterward, I gave her a handwritten thank-you note I wrote just before walking out the door, thanking her for the book interview years prior and that day's conference pass. She gave to the relationship by inviting me to her event, and I supported her and her endeavors through action, keeping our relationship thriving far beyond a single book interview.

In another instance, I had been seeking advice from a successful author who works at my company to learn more about how she balanced writing a book and working full time. We had spoken on the phone and exchanged several emails. I downloaded the sample of her book and read it to get a sense of her topic of expertise, then I sent an email mentioning one word, standout ideas from her writing and asked if she had time to meet during an upcoming company conference. She responded that her time was booked solid. At the conference, I had a break between working sessions during one of her talks and hustled over to hear her speak. Afterward, I waited to meet her and introduced myself in person. We ended up walking together to our next events and sharing experiences author to author. Had I not made it a priority to hear her speak in person and introduce myself, I would not have been able to nurture our formerly brief email and phone interactions into a long-term relationship. I continue to support her writing and engage in conversation in the comments of her social media posts, which are packed with inspiring business insights. Eventually, this relationship would have felt unbalanced because, in our previous interactions, I was mostly seeking advice. In this case, I gave my time and energy to get to know the work that is important to her, and it became clear that we support each other.

Building relationships and focusing on others doesn't require attending conferences or speakers' talks. For example, when I published Adam Lowy's interview on my blog to help tell his story, I added value to his organization and brand. Sharing a colleague's research study, an article they wrote, or their company's job opening on social media, or even passing it on to friends and family through word of mouth, can be simple acts that help you nurture other-centered relationships. Many times, as I'm working to get to know a thought leader's work, like Adam Grant, a Wharton social psychologist and professor whom you'll hear about later, or Jane Dutton, mentioned earlier, I've purchased and read their books and studied their research before reaching out so I could speak in their language. I've downloaded free book samples (often a fifteen-minute exercise) just to get a quick glimpse of their world and show that I've done my research and support them by mentioning key topics they've mastered.

There are so many ways to make a relationship about someone else; the discoveries you'll make can be fascinating once you come from a place of other-centeredness, openness, other-interest, curiosity, care, and exploration of the impact you can make together.

IMPACT

In my workshops, attendees are often amazed that my outreach to high-profile business owners or influential people results in a response. They wonder how I got them to reply. First of all, I don't "get them" to respond—that language is the opposite of other-centeredness and implies a forceful agenda or even, in the worst case, manipulation. In fact, in discussing the title and subtitle of this book, my husband and I got into an involved conversation on whether or not the person "knocking" opens the door, or if the person who has the power to respond to the "knock" does. (Gotta love philosophical dinner conversations—thank you for humoring me, honey.) I believe we have the power to prepare to connect and thoughtfully knock—or reach out to connect with others—and when we do, that may be the first step in opening a previously closed or new door of opportunities with someone. When reaching out for book interviews, whether or not the door was opened by me or the person on the other side, I noticed a pattern in one element of my communications that may have moved them to reply, wanting to engage: highlighting what positive effect, or impact, they can have on a project, cause, or group.

When you're looking to partner with someone, become a representative or an advocate for a group or entity, rather than representing only yourself. As Jessica Malkin, the former CEO of

"Have a purpose; be on purpose. Nothing's more attractive than if someone cares about things, someone who gets passionate and is willing to drumbeat on the floor—fight for a cause—because they are so lit up about it."

—Jessica Malkin

Chicago Ideas, says, "Have a purpose; be on purpose. Nothing's more attractive than if someone cares about things, someone who gets passionate and is willing to drumbeat on the floor—fight for a cause—because they are so lit up about it. Pick an issue, charity, piece of legislation. If you're just singularly passionate about ambition, it's really not that appealing." This relates to our career relationships. If you express that you want a job—any job—it's hard for someone to trust the opinions you share or truly understand you and what's important to you. But if you want a job as a product manager in the health-care tech space because you want to bring best-in-class technology to the medical world to improve patient care, the impact you can make is meaningful. Those you connect with will understand your purpose based on these specifics and that you're pursuing this direction to make a difference for others.

This is why the impact part of Step 2: *Not About Me* is important. But how do we know that the desire to make an impact is what has motivated a contact to respond?

We know because of social impact theory, developed in 1981 by social psychologist and researcher Bibb Latané, PhD, which suggests the person you are reaching out to may be moved to take action or respond if they see a bigger social impact at hand.

Latané's social impact theory includes three things that can cause someone to be influenced to make an impact on others:[15]

1. Personal importance (strength) of the group that they can impact (Example: students at the person's alma mater)

2. Closeness of the group (immediacy), in physical distance and familiarity, that they can impact (Example: students at a local school)

3. Size of the group (number) that they can impact (Example: hundreds of students in a graduating class)

When you bring to light one or more of the three factors above, you may improve your chances that someone will engage with you to partner for a shared goal. Shifting the focus off of your own motives helps to highlight the impact a partnership and collective efforts can make, especially the impact as it relates to what's important to the other person (other-centeredness).

If you're looking to partner with someone, highlight what your work together can do for a higher purpose or for a broader group, particularly one that is important to *them*. So, if you decided to reach out to a role model in your industry who also went to your university (importance and closeness in the form of familiarity) to ask for their time in an informational interview, you might highlight that you would like to publish this interview in the school's newspaper to impart wisdom to the three hundred students in the graduating class (number of people in the group).

If you're looking to partner with someone, highlight what your work together can do for a higher purpose or for a broader group, particularly one that is important to *them*.

Highlighting the impact of your contact taking an action—what it will achieve, especially regarding the importance, the proximity or familiarity, or the size of the group being affected—is critical as you seek to build and foster positive, mutually beneficial career relationships. And, of course, when you highlight impact in a way that the *other* person values (other-centeredness), you're well on your way to opening the door to such relationships. Remember Adam Lowy's story from the beginning of this chapter? To gain buy-in, he shifted from a focus on his goals to the impact Move for Hunger could make by partnering with Wheaton World Wide Moving, and the importance to Wheaton's broad network of agents.

Now, I know this all sounds warm and fuzzy. You've learned

about researching a contact in Step 1. Now, in Step 2: *Not About Me*, you've learned how to reach out thoughtfully to your contact, highlighting the value to them through other-centeredness and the impact they can make with you. Let's say they respond favorably. That's just the start. Now you have the potential to optimize your impact together by maintaining this positive relationship and keeping these concepts at the forefront as your relationship blossoms.

But, why is this critical? Why even go through the extra effort to extensively get to know each individual we forge rich relationships with along our career path, when we could just send a quick LinkedIn message when we need a favor—isn't that what it's there for? What happens if we don't treat each person and relationship with preparation, quality, and care?

Our relationships, our communities, and our economy are at risk of succumbing to shallow interactions that may be easier to execute, yet are more short-lived. When we only serve ourselves, we shortchange ourselves. We make less of an impact on others and stop short of maximizing our opportunities to make a difference or even help future generations. We're not thinking about the bigger picture or strengthening our collective network to lift everyone up to progress further and reach wider.

According to Jane Dutton of the University of Michigan, we get in our own way if we simply focus on professional performance. The social issue of self-centeredness and transactional social interactions goes beyond our personal bubbles—our jobs at our companies in our communities. Tackling larger societal issues like environmental safety or inequality depends on long-term, mutually beneficial partnerships where everyone is valued at every level, beginning with one-on-one, individual interactions. "What will fix it is to unleash human potentiality in humans—meaningful human connection that strengthens and lifts people up," Dutton said.

We are at risk if we take the low road. According to Srikumar S. Rao, author of *Happiness at Work: Be Resilient, Motivated, and Successful—No Matter What*: "If you live the vast majority of your time in a 'me-centered' universe, then you are going to get more than your share of depression, angst, sorrow, and all of the things that make life terrible. That's just the way it is."[16] As you learned in the chapter "How Do You Feel When You Knock?" living in a silo without looking outward and valuing what others bring to the table leads to isolation that can damage your health. So, leave that behind—that's not what we're about here. Here's to living a healthier and more connected life!

HOW DO YOU DO IT?

How do you shift your mindset to others and create impact in a meaningful way for them? You begin by practicing this approach in your own career development interactions. For example, if you are interested in connecting with a leader at a company who has a job you're considering applying to, dive deep into the research about this leader and their company to highlight the impact you can bring to their organization. Say that the company just received an accolade for innovation. You could highlight some innovative ideas you have for their team and the projected impact to the intended audience, and you could mention that you know the company values new ideas. If you follow the company's leader on social media and see that they just spoke at an industry conference on leadership, congratulate them on their recent speaking engagement, tell them you appreciate that the company values participation at industry events, and share the leadership experience you've gained in your current role that you can bring to their team. By doing this, you're also highlighting that you follow the company news and you're already familiar with their work.

Similarly, if someone approaches you about a career conversation, listen. Listen for cues as to how combining your skill sets can make an impact and what's important to them. Try to push back on the instinct to close off, think you're too busy, or question how connecting with them would help you.

> **PRO TIP:** If someone approaches you about a career conversation, listen. Listen for cues as to how combining your skill sets can make an impact and what's important to them. Try to push back on the instinct to close off, think you're too busy, or question how connecting with them would help you.

When you're preparing for interactions and initiating them, use the steps in The Knock Method to research your contact, shift your focus to your contact, bring commonality (overlap and shared interests, covered in Step 4) to the forefront, and highlight the impact and value in their terms. The more you put this into practice with each interaction, the more natural it will become. Soon you won't have to think about it, and the tide will begin to shift. People will feel noticed, like their work matters, and they'll want to engage with you. Everyone's network of relationships will become enriched.

As Wolcott College Prep cofounder Jeff Aeder, whom we met earlier in "A New Way to Knock," said about his quest for believers and supporters in the school: "If those I asked [for financial support for the school] said no, it was because they didn't understand the needs it would serve, and I needed to continue to explain what impact the school would have on others until they understood it. I needed to help them understand the value [impact] they'd be contributing to a cause that needed their support."

You might not resonate with someone new right away, you might get some no's, or you might get some doors opened and then quickly closed when you knock. Don't give up. If something is important to you and you think it could be important to others, too, conduct more research, find common contacts to get to know them and better understand what's important to them, and try again until the impact you can make together begins to emerge.

In the next chapter on Step 3: *Own It*, which explores the value of practicing authenticity, we'll hear from Jenna Benn Shersher. Here's what she said regarding asking for donations and support for her nonprofit organization, Twist Out Cancer, that provides psychosocial support to individuals touched by cancer: "I became a lot more comfortable asking once I realized that what we were doing is making an impact . . . I explain how the community has empowered twenty thousand people to engage."

She isn't asking for donations for herself. Her organization's donors make a financial gift because they feel it will help a broader community of people touched by cancer in some way. They give because of the impact.

Email Example Spotlight

Take a look at the following outreach email example I sent to secure a book interview from Jessica Malkin, former CEO of Chicago Ideas, where I highlighted The Knock Method steps woven throughout. Take special note of Step 2: *Not About Me* and the focus on her work and impact. *Email is slightly edited for privacy and accuracy.*

Email Subject Line: Hello from a Chicago Ideas Supporter
Hi Jessica,

*I'm reaching out as **a big fan of Chicago Ideas.** [Not About Me, Other-Centeredness] I've attended five-plus events, including CIW [Chicago Ideas Week] and presentations by Deepak Chopra and Adam Grant! I'm so impressed with Chicago Ideas' event production and programming, and the ability for it to unite the Chicago community and beyond and open our minds, hearts, and creativity. [Not About Me, Other-Centeredness, Impact]*

*I recently moved from Chicago to Denver, and in fact, it looks like we have **several mutual connections in Chicago from LinkedIn, including [Person A], [Person B], and [Person C]. [Research, Commonality]***

*I'm writing my first book about building lasting career relationships and partnerships through human connection, featuring interviews from **CIW speakers [Other-Centeredness]** Adam Grant and Move for Hunger's founder, Adam Lowy. In fact, **CIW inspired me to reach out for these interviews [Impact]** and I was honored they said yes!*

*As the CEO of Chicago Ideas leading programming and development, would you be open to an interview for my book to **share how you continue to build the CIW brand, impact, and partnerships, bringing together so many creative minds and successful people to foster innovation? [Not About Me, Other-Centeredness]***

Your interview will be featured alongside advice [Impact] about building quality relationships from many others who have built something from the ground up, including:

- *The founder of a high school for kids with learning challenges in Chicago—Wolcott College Prep*

- *A film producer and apparel brand founder*

- *A CEO of a major food company in Chicago*

- *The founder of an art therapy cancer support nonprofit*

continued

> • *The director of the Anti-Defamation League's Civil Rights Policy Planning Center*
>
> *Would you be available for a brief phone conversation one morning around 9 a.m. in the next week?*
> *I look forward to hearing from you.*

Similarly, I was nervous to reach out to Adam Grant, a best-selling author, researcher, and TED speaker I admire.[17] I had the privilege of interviewing him four years before, and I wanted to reconnect to share how his advice had helped students and professionals in The Knock Method workshops, and ask for feedback. He had gained popularity and become a more accomplished author since then, and I doubted myself because so much time had passed, and questioned whether he would even see my note or make the time to respond. I used the following email subject line, highlighting impact:

> **SUBJECT: Follow-Up: Your 2014 interview has helped 50+ students and professionals!**

> And, sure enough, Adam Grant replied and connected me with a member of his research team for feedback on The Knock Method. He's always finding ways to be generous. You'll learn more about how he does this to help his community—which is vast—in Chapter 5.

NOT ABOUT ME:
KEY TIPS TO APPLY THIS STEP

Here is a list of ways you can adjust your interactions with career contacts to shift the focus off of yourself and onto them and what you can achieve together.

- **Open the door to collaborate, rather than starting with an ask.** Instead of asking a contact, especially a new contact, for something right away, think about opening the door to a collaboration by focusing on what's important to them and why you're reaching out to *them* specifically. Don't go into a conversation or meeting expecting to get something from them, even if you have a goal in mind. Simply make time to connect, share, and discover each other, which can establish a longer-term foundation on which to build a mutually beneficial relationship rather than a transactional one.

- **Tailor communications based on your research about another person.** Use the research you conducted in Step 1: *Know My Topic and My Contact* to tailor communications to focus on your contact and bring to light the impact based on what they value.

- **Use time before a meeting to prepare personal conversation points.** When you're on your way to a meeting with a contact, use the transit time or few minutes before a virtual meeting to think about something they shared last time you connected online, or something you know from a mutual contact. Have conversation starters specific to them ready. Then, ask about these things to show you were listening and have an interest in them.

- **Put meeting times in the other person's time zone.** When finding time to connect with a contact by phone or by appointment, put potential meeting times in *their* time zone to make it easy for them to accept and set a date without having to fumble over logistics. If you don't know it, research it online, on their website bio, or LinkedIn profile, or ask a mutual contact.

- **Use the other person's perceived preferred mode of communication (use your best guess).** Try to use your contact's preferred mode of communication. For example, if they're very active on Twitter, consider following along to get a sense of what they like to share; and when it's time to connect, maybe sending a direct message is the way to go. Or you might have their personal email from another contact, but you want to ensure you don't catch them off guard in their personal inbox, so you send a professional note to their work email. If they're speaking at a conference, consider attending so you can meet them after their presentation and mention ideas they shared that resonated with you. Some of the people I interviewed for this book prefer to keep in contact over text—such as a busy restaurateur—others through Instagram messages, and others via email. I tried to go for their preferred channels to accommodate their communications needs.

- **Highlight the impact to another person in email subject lines.** Make email subject lines about something of value to *them*. For example, "One of your biggest supporters," "Your interview has impacted X number of people," "Help us support 500 students this year."

- **Research through commonality to personalize communications *for them*.** Find someone you have in common with the person you'd like to connect with, and ask them about your potential contact: What is their work style like? How would you describe their personality? Are they a coffee or a tea person? Anything specific I should mention or not mention to them? Then, you're set up to craft a message that speaks to them (other-centeredness) and what is important to them (impact).

- **Consider personal interests and lifestyle to make connecting easier for the other person.** If appropriate and available, get to know your contact's lifestyle and family life. If they have young children, suggesting early-morning meetings may be tricky due to school drop-off; or maybe they take an annual vacation in the same month, so be prepared to work around it by suggesting meeting times before or after that month.

- **Relate on important causes.** Through your online research, such as news interviews, social media, or company bios, you may learn about philanthropic causes that are important to them. Mention connections you may have to similar causes, or simply say that you both have causes that are important to you. After you connect, consider making a donation to the organizations important to your contact as a thank-you.

- **Jot down notes to keep personal relationships going.** Keep a log of individuals you are connecting with, whether you're searching for a job, seeking startup partners or investors, or reaching out to contacts that came recommended by a colleague. Then, make note of any personal details you may want to remember later to keep interactions personal and memorable. Similarly, mention key topics you discussed in a follow-up note, then review your past emails next time you're preparing to connect with that contact again as a refresher and to follow up on updates during the next meeting.

PRO TIP: Your inbox can serve as a helpful memory log for intentionally connecting in your career.

\ | /

3

OWN IT

Be personal and authentic; invest in the
relationship and the cause up front

This is the confidence chapter! Whether you're at a loss
for what step to take next on your career path, or you're
not quite sure of the best way to reach out to that leader
in your organization for mentoring advice, you're about to feel
much better about that uncertainty.

Confidence is fundamental to building quality relationships.
But nobody teaches you how to effectively navigate relationships
at various career stages. How do you get the experience that's listed
in the job description? How do you make the leap to a new area
of interest without the formal training that other candidates have?
This kind of uncertainty creates fear. Fear blocks your path to confidence, which prevents you from taking the leap, putting yourself
out there, reaching out to someone new, or pursuing a new career.
You need a safety net for feeling more confident and maximizing
opportunities, rather than missing out on them. For that, lean on
The Knock Method.

Take inspiration from the stories that follow about professionals who pushed through (or bypassed) fear and accomplished great things. You'll gain confidence and reassurance that when building relationships, if you showcase your true self and put in the work, you can unlock boundless opportunities in your career and beyond. At a minimum, you'll progress further than where you are now and learn something. Hello, growth!

Let's start with an inspiring example of how authenticity opened the door to making a world of difference for thousands of people touched by cancer.

BRING YOUR GUARD DOWN AND OTHERS WILL TOO: BUILDING TRUST THROUGH AUTHENTICITY

Jenna Benn Shersher didn't pause to weigh her options—she didn't have that choice.

At the age of twenty-nine, Jenna, genuine and sweet-natured, would have rather focused on building her career and living up her social life in Chicago. But she was diagnosed with a rare form of lymphoma, one that affects fewer than three hundred people in the United States.

She felt marginalized. As she received treatment, she was forced to stay alone in her bedroom because her immune system was compromised. But her instinct was to not give in to isolation, to not hold back, to not think about what-ifs, and to not conjure up fears of what others would think. Instead of hiding, she did the opposite. She yearned for community and connectedness, so she put herself out there—online.

Despite her fear, she found confidence by tapping into her innate love of dance and a compulsion to connect with others. With no motive other than to be herself, she brought others into *her* world by sharing videos of herself dancing, doing the twist on social media channels. She invited friends to send videos of themselves dancing too and received an outpouring of love and support, with many mirroring her unrivaled, unapologetic gumption. She gave others permission to move their bodies in whatever ways moved *them*, and soon all of this activity blossomed into a growing social media community on YouTube and Facebook. Although it wasn't planned, Jenna found herself celebrating vulnerability, exemplifying fearlessness, and personifying authenticity.

And then she realized she could do even more.

As soon as she had completed her cancer treatment, Jenna created Twist Out Cancer,[1] a nonprofit that provides psychosocial support to individuals touched by cancer, support expressed through creative arts programming, not just dance but visual arts and more. Twist Out Cancer's cornerstone event series, Brushes with Cancer, pairs those "brushed with" (touched by) cancer with artists who depict their stories and then display their work at an art showcase, celebrating life and those facing adversity. Twist Out Cancer has reached more than thirty thousand people in eight cities across the world: Ann Arbor, Michigan; Austin, Texas; Chicago; Detroit; Philadelphia; Tel Aviv, Israel; and Toronto and Montreal, Canada. The nonprofit's online community has generated a donor base of more than nine thousand people and over thirty thousand program supporters. In 2020 alone, Twist Out Cancer raised more than $850,000, with an outstanding 85 percent going directly to events and programs that help its community.

How has Jenna been able to inspire such support? Through her authenticity. "This community was built not with any intention. It came out of a raw, desperate place, when I was being open and honest in my experiences," she told me. "Because I allowed myself to be vulnerable, because I was being so raw about everything, people felt they could connect to me. Without any reservations, I just put myself out there."

How does she get that buy-in for others to say they're willing to trust her? "Bring your guard down and others will," she said. By having the confidence to showcase her openness and authenticity, even when she was isolated and afraid, Jenna has assembled a broad, inclusive community. Members are more empowered and feel safe they are able to share too.

Jenna successfully runs the nonprofit and raises funds with a team of only three people. Unflinching, she just about bypasses the fear many face in asking for money, career support, or even simply to connect for a casual career conversation.

Rejection is part of any growth process, including your career. "If you're in fundraising, you have to know you're going to make asks, and reach out and write grants, and get a lot of rejection letters along with the yeses," Jenna said. "The worst thing that happens is that they say no."

Jenna grew thick skin through sharing her vulnerable story and embracing her authenticity. She learned to advocate on behalf of a broader community in need of support and knew that she could progress further by showing up rather than succumbing to fear, even in the face of inevitable rejection.

"You will fail," she explained. "It's like throwing darts. Eventually you'll hit the target." Showing up with this kind of confidence and perseverance to a job search, a networking event, or a review meeting at work to discuss a promotion can help

> **"Bring your guard down and others will."**
>
> —Jenna Benn Shersher

you progress. While separating herself from unsuccessful asks and not taking rejection as a personal attack has been a big challenge,

Jenna has learned not to take it personally. After all, it's a business decision, she says.

HOW JENNA KNOCKS

Jenna was successful because she *owned it*. She claimed and exposed her own vulnerability. Even when she was isolated, which can create negative health risks as the research showed in the chapter, "How Do You Feel When You Knock?" she learned that cultivating human connections when you are vulnerable counteracts loneliness and attracts others. She showed up as her most authentic self. She demonstrated fearlessness by putting herself out there even when she was isolated.

Jenna believes that when you let your guard down with authenticity, others will too. It makes the interaction more relatable and builds trust and human connection. She knows she is going to get rejected and has gotten used to it because it's part of the process, but she shows up with confidence anyway. And while rejection never feels good, it's a lot better than living in fear of it and never trying to progress.

THE KNOCK METHOD STEP 3 IN ACTION

Own it (Authenticity)	Revealed her vulnerable self and invited others in. When she opened up, others did too.

If Jenna can own it during one of her most fearful, vulnerable, and isolated times, we all owe it to ourselves to have the confidence to at least try by revealing who we are, even in moments of weakness, as we approach unfamiliar people and territory and truly connect with others along our careers. Being vulnerable when we knock can open more doors than hiding in fear behind closed ones.

Authenticity is only part of the equation that helps build trust in relationships. It works best paired with making an investment in others: individuals and organizations you might collaborate with. Investing in relationships is about demonstrating positive intention through action. When someone takes action, expending time or energy toward an interaction or relationship with you, and when they are genuine, personable, and maybe even vulnerable, you will trust them and the situation more, and it's more likely you'll feel comfortable taking the next step.

This happens not just in the nonprofit world, but in sales too. That's what Rick Otis demonstrated when he found himself in another unlikely setting for giving financial advice.

HOW A FINANCIAL ADVISOR INVESTS IN NEW RELATIONSHIPS

Would you invite an insurance salesman into your hot tub?

That's the question that three lounging guests in the Jacuzzi at the Phoenix Marriott might have asked themselves as Rick Otis approached and asked, "Will you let a Texas guy in?"

Rick, a perpetually engaging athleisure enthusiast and top-ranked financial advisor with MassMutual, rarely goes anywhere without his Texas Longhorns hat. He was out of his territory when visiting Arizona for a conference, so he needed to find a way to start the conversation before immersing himself in close quarters (and shared waters) with what turned out to be college football rivals.

They asked Rick what he did for a living. Eventually one of the guests admitted, "I hate my financial advisor." Rick offered to help. The man seemed unsure. Then, he began to ask Rick about pricing and scenarios for some financial services and products. Rick stopped to think before replying, even though he was usually generous with his expertise.

The reason: the prospect was from Illinois. Rick lives up to the strict financial advising ethical guidelines. "I make sure to do everything correctly to protect my license—both to protect my career and to help others with their finances in an honest way," he said. "I was afraid to talk to him about his financial matters before I was licensed to conduct business in his state." He wasn't confident or prepared to make the business conversation official, and fear crept in.

But he decided to invest in the relationship, so he took the steps to prepare himself and build trust with the prospect.

"I got out of the pool, dried off, took the elevator to my hotel room, logged on to my computer, and applied and paid for a license to practice in Illinois, which was $210," Rick recalled. "I went back to the hot tub and potential client and said, 'I can at least talk to you now because I'm licensed in Illinois.'"

Then he found out that while the guy was from Illinois, he lived in Ohio, so Rick dried off again, went *back* upstairs, and got licensed in Ohio for $50 before resuming the conversation.

Does that sound like an over-the-top effort just to have a conversation? As Rick said: "The client ended up buying five insurance policies over the years, and I've only met him once. I talk to him every couple months, but I only met him once at the pool."

HOW RICK KNOCKS

Here's why Rick was successful in turning a poolside conversation into a long-term business relationship.

To address his lack of confidence, feel more prepared, and live up to his ethical standard, he interrupted the conversation to immediately gain the right license to help the prospect before discussing financial matters. He made an investment in the relationship from the start (personally, not monetarily). His actions proved he was committed to—or invested in—immersing himself in his client's life and not just the shared hot tub, so he could ultimately help him better.

You may be thinking, sure, he did what it took to get the sale. But his actions proved otherwise. Not everyone would have done the due diligence and put in the time to thoughtfully ensure they were legally authorized to help their prospect, especially in a casual setting.

Investing in relationships is about preparation. When you're prepared, you're more confident to take action toward a mutually beneficial partnership with an individual or group. You can say you're interested in partnering with someone, but how do you *show* them? Bring something to the table that you believe would be of value to them, as I illustrated in the chapter, "How Do You Feel When You Knock?" Remember that I put together a list of resources my work team had created before meeting with the product team so they had a better sense of what I was describing for a more productive conversation.

Contribute to the relationship up front. What actions can you take that answer these questions for your contact: Why should I engage with this person, individual, company, or cause? Is it worth my time? Are there good intentions present? What impact will meeting with this person have on others? Why *me* rather than others they can partner with? Do I feel good about their character?

THE KNOCK METHOD STEP 3 IN ACTION

Own it (Investment)	Put in the extra work up front to prepare and build trust.

OWN IT: THIS STEP IN CONTEXT

Step 3: *Own It* in The Knock Method is about showing up to professional relationships with confidence. The Knock Method exists in part to build confidence by helping people during transitional or growth phases in their careers.

When you find yourself approaching a career transition like the examples in the following list, remember that these are natural times when it's most appropriate and helpful to boost the number and quality of relationships.

- Taking your career to the next level (*career growers*)

- Starting a career or even a startup venture (*career builders*)

- Changing jobs or careers (*career changers*)

Think of it this way. We have building/growing phases and doing phases of our careers. Imagine yourself climbing a mountain. When you are building your career, you're on your way up to a new opportunity (or over—growth isn't always up, it can mean deepening your expertise, or making a lateral move over to a new team at the same level). Similarly, when you're growing, you're on your way up (or over) again to the next role or opportunity. When you are doing, you're on a plateau, learning on the job, mastering a new skill set, or familiarizing yourself with your team and role. To clarify, when you're doing, you're certainly not stagnant because you're learning, working with others, and putting your skills to work. But the purpose of this concept is that you grow into opportunities, and then grow *in* them, paying attention to the transition times. Between steps, you're at a junction, before you make a move. During these pivotal moments, there should be spikes in the number and quality of relationships you develop. Then, once you make a move, you can nurture and give to those relationships at turning points along the way. As you develop your career, you'll grow a wider, richer network of quality relationships that are more valuable for everyone involved.

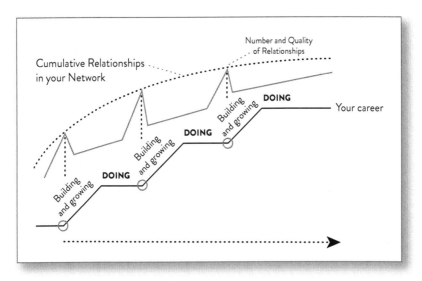

Figure 3.1—The interactions between the building, growing, and doing phases of a career.

When you feel confusion or fear about how to take the next step in your career, put your energy into expanding your network to gather information, finding ways to partner with others, and focusing on what you can give to relationships and your network. This way, you're taking steps forward and creating career growth for yourself and others. Remember, build relationships because of

When you feel confusion or fear about how to take the next step in your career, put your energy into expanding your network to gather information, finding ways to partner with others, and focusing on what you can give to relationships and your network.

what you can give and contribute to them, not for what you want, need, or can take.

For example, if you're looking to change roles within your company because you can apply more of your skill set and passion on a different team, you could increase the number of individuals you connect with on other teams to confirm your intuition. Then, keep in touch with them as you work toward taking the next step in your career.

During career transitions, when we approach new or unfamiliar territory, we often lack confidence. Step 3: *Own It* is designed to empower you to combat your natural reaction to retreat when you find yourself nearing unfamiliar waters, and instead go toward them by intentionally showing up with your authentic self and investing in potential relationships and opportunities through action and showing commitment.

Here's an example from my own career where I learned the value of practicing authenticity and having confidence when building career relationships.

After working with small businesses, nonprofits, and startups during most of my twenties, I decided I wanted to contribute to the marketing industry in a bigger way. I knew I could make more of an impact for bigger brands and their customers, with wider footprints, and gain experience from marketing agencies, companies, and marketers who were at the forefront of the industry. I hoped to gain knowledge and credibility in my profession by working on more complex business challenges with the power to have more significant results.

Going into the job search, I was missing marketing experience with large brands, and so I was missing confidence too. One day, I interviewed at a large, well-respected marketing agency. While I was confident about my resume and my career that landed me the interview, having previously built my own company centered around marketing for small businesses, I was less confident about how to navigate questions about making this change to larger accounts.

While I *owned it*—and demonstrated authenticity—by stating this would be new for me, I must have also shown some insecurity, and my interviewer noticed. His reaction surprised me. "I don't see the lack of big-company experience as a negative," he said. "I think that if you were able to convince small family-owned businesses and startups with shallow pockets [where they're protective about where they spend their money] to hire your company for marketing, then certainly, you have a lot to offer big brands with deep pockets." He changed my perspective completely! He saw my ability to showcase value for people and companies on tight marketing budgets and perceived that as a potential asset for his company. Authenticity can be an asset, and showcasing who you are and your unique experience can set you apart and help you build quality relationships along your career. *Own it.* Know that your experience and effort are worthy of an opportunity. Be yourself and use it to stand out.

Here's another example when authenticity came into play in a job interview for me.

When I interviewed for a marketing consulting role at a tech company a little later in my career, I had detailed and broad experience across marketing channels for an extensive client portfolio in most digital channels—social media, web marketing, content marketing, search engine marketing, and public relations. But email marketing was one channel I had less experience with. At the end of my phone interview, I asked the interviewer, "Are there any gaps in my experience we haven't talked about yet that I can speak to?"

This is one of the most valuable questions to gauge your standing at the end of an interview and create an opportunity to ease remaining doubts.

Basically, I was asking if there were any outstanding questions in his mind about me being the right fit for the role. He replied honestly, sharing that the position was heavily focused on email marketing and that my experience was lighter in this channel, but that customers were increasingly asking about content (messaging) strategy, an area I had developed expertise in and that could really be of value to the team. We uncovered that email was an area I could learn more about, given my otherwise well-rounded marketing experience. In the end, we had an honest, authentic conversation about gaps and learning opportunities, and he offered me the job, which I accepted. He took a chance I could come up to speed on the email channel, and I took the same chance, knowing that I had to work doubly hard to catch up with my peers, but also, that I could come to the team with confidence, offering a unique set of skills.

> **PRO TIP:** At the end of a job interview, if time allows, ask something like this to get a sense of your standing and an opportunity to speak to any remaining doubts: "Are there any gaps in my experience we haven't talked about yet that I can speak to?"

OWN IT: OPENING THE DOOR TO THIS STEP

Reminder: This step is about authenticity—embracing who you are and showcasing it—which pairs well with investment or showing your commitment to a potential relationship through action.

THE KNOCK METHOD
Five steps to open doors and build relationships that matter

High-quality relationship: A mutually beneficial collaboration where both parties contribute and the outcome is stronger	
Know my topic, my contact, and specifics up front. Prepare to connect.	**Research/Specifics**
Not about me. Focus on my contacts, us, and our mutual impact.	**Other-Centeredness/ Impact**
Own it. Be personal and authentic; invest in the relationship and the cause up front.	**Authenticity/ Investment**
Commonality. Build trust to open the door.	**Commonality**
Keep giving. Help others and practice generosity and gratitude.	**Generosity/ Gratitude**

AUTHENTICITY: DON'T BE AN IMPOSTER TO YOURSELF OR TO OTHERS

Authenticity often means exposing our own vulnerabilities (which, I know, sounds terrifying). Practicing authenticity also makes us more approachable and relatable, and demonstrates that we're all human. When building relationships, it pays to share personal details when appropriate and share more about who we are— our hopes, fears, dreams, challenges, and successes—because it's likely that others can empathize or relate. As we learned from Jenna Benn Shersher, the more we open up, the more others will too, creating an opportunity for more high-quality relationships that have staying power. While the stories and examples I've already shared show that it works, what does science say about why authenticity is so important?

As it turns out, one perspective is that our psychological well-being—or having a healthy mindset—depends on us being true to ourselves and behaving in ways that are consistent with our values and morals. One powerful study from the research team of Francesca Gino, Maryam Kouchaki, and Adam Galinsky highlights that when we don't act in accordance with what we feel and believe—when we're not authentic or true to ourselves— we may feel immoral.[2] We might even feel physically dirty, like we need to clean up, for example, by taking a shower. And, when we feel we've gone against our gut, we feel we need to behave in ways that help others in order to counteract this inauthenticity. Better to act in the best interest of others and ourselves from the get-go, rather than to compensate for actions that aren't genuine.

Authenticity in action is twofold:

1. How you present yourself to others

2. How well your actions align with your own morals, values, and beliefs

After getting to know The Knock Method, you'll feel better equipped to shift focus off of yourself through other-centeredness when building relationships, but also in ways that are authentic to who you are, knowing that it's better for yourself and for your interactions with others.

Over the past few years, the concept of "imposter syndrome," or feeling unqualified for a job, career, task, or office culture, has surfaced. And, of course, it has to do with confidence.

I was assigned a project in my first job out of college to lead a large government technology proposal document worth hundreds of thousands of dollars. I thought, "Why would someone entrust me with a large project at work with so much money at stake? What if I fail or don't live up to the company's standards?" Fear crept in—that familiar obstacle to confidence. I glazed over the fact that I wouldn't have been given the responsibility—along with a team and leaders to support me—if the company didn't trust me with the project and didn't feel my skill set was appropriate for the required level of work. My background, proven work ethic, and maybe even my personality—who I was—were enough. My authentic self received a high level of responsibility because I was worthy and capable, and had the support of my team and leadership if I needed it, and I should have been more confident. I delivered the project with the highest quality that I could, and it paid off. I then had more confidence for the next project that came across my desk.

But what about being an imposter to ourselves—not being authentic or acting in congruence with what we believe? The Association for Psychological Science says, "Being an imposter to oneself leads to moral and psychological distress."[3] It's better for our body and our minds and for those we're connecting with to just be ourselves.

So, while you're out there building confidence, stretching beyond your fear zone, and building and nurturing relationships to further your career, remember that being true to yourself and authentic when you show up around others is not only a successful career development strategy, it's also better for your mental health.

HOW DO YOU DO IT?

You may be thinking, "I already am behaving in a way that shows who I am. How do I learn to be more authentic?" Practicing authenticity in career interactions and relationships is about bringing more of who you are to the forefront. It has to do with being personal, admitting when you don't know the answer to a question (but you'll research it to find out), or sharing your fears or doubts about a particular opportunity or subject. It may even mean admitting to yourself that an opportunity doesn't feel like the right fit for *you*—and sharing that after further interviews and conversations. We're often so caught up in the interview process, worried about whether a company wants to hire us, that we often don't slow down to do our own work to confirm that the job is worth pursuing. To get hired, you may find yourself trying to paint a picture for your future that fits the job description, when in fact, the job isn't a fit and you wouldn't ultimately be happy in that role. Being honest with yourself and with others in career relationships and as you develop your career will serve you, your teammates, and likely even your company better. Building relationships with an open mind and giving them breathing room to see how they develop may help you discover exciting opportunities and move on from the not-such-a-great-fit ones.

Building relationships with an open mind and giving them breathing room to see how they develop may help you discover exciting opportunities and move on from the not-such-a-great-fit ones.

Career Changer Example: Let's say you're a nurse and you're considering changing careers to work in marketing. Tap into the authenticity part of Step 3: *Own It.* A lack of confidence may creep in because you feel you're vying for the same jobs with those who are trained in marketing, and your nursing career isn't exactly relevant experience on paper. Here comes the human component— you need to be yourself. Use a pinch of creativity to relate the two fields and exemplify transferable skill sets, or qualifications in one role that you can apply to another, even if they might seem unrelated at first.

When you connect with contacts in the marketing industry, you might even give an example of an epic day—when and how you handled several difficult cases and resolved each patient's issue, going home knowing you made a difference—to highlight the care you'd bring to your marketing clients. You can still demonstrate authenticity and showcase who you are, confident in your story about coming from a completely different industry, even when the job requirements say otherwise. Authenticity pays off and opens the door to opportunities, and it combines well with investment—putting in the work, especially when it comes to boosting knowledge and experience in a new field, or going from point A to point B in your career.

INVESTMENT

Whether you find yourself in a situation for a potential new partnership, or you initiate communication with someone on your career path, making an investment in relationships even before they begin shows your intentions up front and that you're willing to put the work in. Investment is also about showcasing accountability and that you see it as your responsibility to work for the relationship. For example, if you're reaching out to a family friend about a job opportunity at their company, take the time to familiarize yourself with the company's website, news, and other job opportunities, and be able to explain what you can bring to the company and that particular role. Showcasing your commitment through action makes connecting with you worth your family friend's time. It can also help boost their perceived value at work, if they

Making an investment in relationships even before they begin shows your intentions up front and that you're willing to put the work in.

bring in talent (you) that can improve the organization. Similarly, if a friend goes out of their way to introduce you to someone about a career opportunity, make sure to follow through on the introduction, or you might be damaging your reputation and your friend's.

HOW DO YOU DO IT?

For *career changers*, the investment component of Step 3 is one of my favorite strategies for exploring what it would be like if you make a career move from point A to point B. It's a great way to get unstuck if you're in a role and you want to pursue another one. Investment reduces uncertainty and fear about what point B would be like and replaces it with knowledge, expertise, and confidence.

Let's continue with our nursing-to-marketing *career changer* example. You might feel unqualified, timid, and afraid to pursue roles in a completely new career. You lack confidence because that would be a big jump!

So, how do you shorten the distance or make the gap smaller between where you are (point A) and where you'd like to be (point B)? According to Adam Galinsky in his TED talk, "How to Speak Up for Yourself," one way to boost that confidence and bring more to the bargaining table, or feel worthy of a task, job, or opportunity, is to beef up your expertise.[4] And to do that, you take action to show your commitment, gaining knowledge in the process.

You talk to several professional marketers to get a sense of their day-to-day role. You watch marketing videos online and subscribe to marketing blogs so you can familiarize yourself with the industry. You sign up to volunteer at a marketing conference so you can meet others in the field and soak up knowledge between your nursing shifts. You might even take a part-time class or a virtual course on marketing so you boost your knowledge of the field. After careful consideration and months of immersing yourself in their world, you know that the connection, customer service, and creative parts of marketing are skills you used every day as a nurse. You had to immediately build rapport with new patients every twelve-hour shift. You had to think on the spot when the nurse call button rang for a variety of issues. Building connection was about building trust through helping patients—or customer service—but in health care, rather than marketing.

Once you've immersed yourself in the industry and confirmed you do, in fact, want to make this career shift, you have some education under your belt and *own it*—exude authenticity when you show up for informational interviews or it comes time to write your cover letter for a job. Furthermore, you become familiar with the industry's terminology, challenges, and trends, so you can speak to why you're interested in making this change. Most of all, you've made an investment in the field, through time and energy, which will give you confidence. This career switch went from being just an idea and something unlikely to happen to a more formalized option that you've validated through the effort you've put in.

Investing yourself can give you experience where you have none, which can be especially helpful for *career changers*, as well as for *career builders* and *career growers*. It shortens the gap between point A and point B.

Email Example Spotlight

Here's an email I wrote to Wharton professor, author, and organizational psychologist Adam Grant to try to secure an interview with him for my book. I spent forty-five minutes on it, conducting research, being other-centered, and bringing impact to the forefront, to try to get it just right. Of those I reached out to for book interviews, he was the furthest from me in terms of being in the same social sphere; he also had the highest profile of those I reached out to for book interviews. After forty-eight hours, when I had convinced myself I wouldn't hear back, he replied, offering one of his open calendar times for a phone call, which he offers to people like me in his community who prove to him there's mutual value in meeting. I was thrilled! And I had more proof that connecting intentionally with others, using the steps in The Knock Method, pays off and creates value for both individuals. *Email is slightly edited for privacy and accuracy.*

May 2014
Subject Line: Your Newest Give and Take *Reader!*
Hi Adam,
*I'm a social media strategist, blogger, and relationship builder in Chicago, and **the newest reader (and fan!) of** Give and Take. [Not About Me, Other-Centeredness, Research, Investment] I'm about one-third in and I'm hooked—I'll never look at an executive headshot without analyzing facial expressions again!*

Through Give and Take, not only am I learning about real-world cases of Givers, Takers, and Matchers and evaluating which role I take on most

continued

often, I'm also learning tips for book content structure and flow from you.
[Investment, Authenticity]

I'm currently writing my first book about the idea that we all need and rely on the support and help of others to be successful, and the importance of building relationships before asking for their help—to maximize the benefit for everyone. **Instead of focusing on giving only to receive (as a Taker or Matcher might do), [Other-Centeredness]** it shows that thoughtful steps like conducting audience research, understanding their values, and giving to the relationship over time can make asking colleagues, role models, and even strangers for help easier and more fruitful.

I'd love to interview you for my book, **as a successful professor and author, about how you've asked others for help along your journey and how you help others too. I'm also curious if you've conducted research that supports my ideas that I could reference? [Impact, Giving]**

I am excited to attend your Chicago Ideas Week talk in June! **[Research, Investment, Not About Me]** Would you be available to **meet when you are in town [Research, Commonality]** to share an experience or two? At a minimum, I'd love to **share feedback on Give and Take and learn about your writing process [Giving, Generosity]** since I am a new author.

I look forward to hearing from you—have a great week!

Rebecca

P.S. If you need any Chicago restaurant "Rebeccammendations," happy to help! [Giving, Generosity]

Who else is owning it, practicing authenticity, and taking action to invest in relationships?

"My approach [to building professional relationships] is a bit more like friendship," said Andy Crestodina, the cofounder of Orbit Media Studios and author of *Content Chemistry*.[5] In fact, after he received a review blurb for the cover of his book from Jay Baer, founder of the marketing consulting firm Convince & Convert, Andy sent him a pricey bottle of tequila, knowing Jay is a tequila fan. Sharing who you are—your likes, dislikes, lifestyle, family, struggles, and previous job experiences—gives others personal ways to connect with you and transform what could have been serious professional relationships into professional friendships.

> **"My approach [to building professional relationships] is a bit more like friendship."**
>
> —Andy Crestodina

This kind of interaction is the goal of The Knock Method. Building positive, high-quality relationships creates an experience, not an exchange. It's not about this for that or ending a generous gesture with, "Let me know if there's anything I can do to help you out in the future," even though cordial, appreciated, and encouraged. It's about investing time and energy, up front and on an ongoing basis, in the relationship so that you already know how you can add value for your contacts before an interaction and continue to add value as you would in a long-term friendship. The same can be said for influencer partnerships with companies and brands. Remember in the chapter, "A New Way to Knock," when I shared how brands were reaching out for a quick mention on my blog? It felt one-sided and more like an exchange of text on websites

> **Building positive, high-quality relationships creates an experience, not an exchange.**

without any feeling. I was craving an experience, one that I could see, touch, feel, or taste—one that would have created a richer partnership and possibly an interactive opportunity for my readers with that brand.

I learned more about how to approach career opportunities and relationships with confidence when I went to hear Julie Smolyansky, CEO of Lifeway Foods, speak at a conference, as I described in Chapter 2. Although the interaction came naturally, it was no coincidence that I continued to make an investment in our relationship by attending her event. In an earlier interview, she had told me, "I do think it's a little bit hard to cold call somebody out of the blue. Not in a creepy, stalkerish way, but if I'm promoting an event, the best time to connect with me is when I'm hosting a fundraising event—buy a ticket." She made herself available in just those kinds of public settings. So that's how I reconnected with her.

> ## "I do think it's a little bit hard to cold call somebody out of the blue. Not in a creepy, stalkerish way, but if I'm promoting an event, the best time to connect with me is when I'm hosting a fundraising event—buy a ticket."
>
> —Julie Smolyansky

Instead of taking time out of her day for one-on-one coffee meetings, she finds it helpful when someone invests in the relationship by keeping up to date with her projects and making the effort to go to an event she's promoted and find her there.

Think of this professional relationship as you would one with a friend—you check in with them, you catch up on their social media posts, and you congratulate them on their achievements. You both give to the friendship to invest in each other and mutually benefit.

Julie added, "I appreciate when someone is considerate of an individual's time. I do the same thing. When I'm trying to reach someone, I'll go to their TED talk or another venue or conference they are speaking at and find them there, as one way to establish a relationship. And I don't go there with an ask." She said she may be investing in, and establishing, a relationship for five years before an opportunity comes up where she's asking for anything.

What about authenticity and tackling fear through building confidence?

"In terms of getting over fear, make yourself uncomfortable. If you're not letting fear in, you're not reaching high enough. I try to do things—physical exercises that force me to get uncomfortable and go past my fear. That is a bravery muscle you can flex and get stronger at until it feels more comfortable," Julie said.

Jessica Malkin, former CEO of Chicago Ideas, said authenticity speaks to her. She has built a network of rich relationships by helping others in an authentic way and sees this way of living like cultivating a garden of seeds and connections that will blossom into opportunities for everyone. "Come to a relationship with some level of authentic selflessness and realize there will be a day when as a leader, or in your personal life, you will need something," she said. "The more opportunities people open themselves up to with vulnerability, the easier it is to help other people." Being vulnerable and open gives others the confidence to open up in return.

As you consider that next career step or connection, use The Knock Method as your reminder to be authentic when helping others, plant seeds that build a strong network of connections that look a bit more like friendship for years to come, and do something that makes you feel uncomfortable to grow confidence. Lean on The Knock Method when you need some inspiring stories or how-tos when pushing past your own fears.

Here are ways you can embrace your authenticity and invest in relationships to develop your career:

- **Time:** Take the time to attend speaker presentations and events to connect with others in person, to support them, and to get to know their areas of expertise.

- **Action:** Purchase books or download digital previews from authors and professionals you may be looking to connect with. Read their research. Watch their videos. Invest yourself in the relationship by supporting their work. Buy their product so you can share your thoughts as a customer and supporter.

- **Stay connected:** Stay connected through social media channels, email, and in person to know if someone in your network is traveling near you. Keep up to date on your contacts' projects and events so you can jump on opportunities to see and support them, which may mean sharing their cause with your network.

- **Be yourself:** This is important, especially in communications with others you don't know well. Share photos of when you met in outreach emails, or mention your biggest takeaway from their presentation. Remind your contact of where you met or who/what you have in common, and reveal something about yourself related to them. Here are some examples I've used: "I'm the newest reader of your book, and here's one thing I took away from it" or "I've already started incorporating your cookbook into my kitchen."

- **Share your professional experience with confidence:** In career conversations and job interviews, highlight how your experience and skills might be transferable to a different clientele or role, even when it may seem different on paper. Use what you've learned when you put in the work to show your commitment and contributions to a specific opportunity or relationship.

- **Feed the friendship:** When a relationship becomes mutually beneficial and long term, it becomes more natural and more like friendship. Stay up to date, and keep in touch with your network of high-quality career contacts through social media, individual emails, calls, and catch-up sessions; share important work of others with your network; and know that the more work you put into relationships, the more they will grow.

OWN IT:
KEY TIPS TO APPLY THIS STEP

Authenticity

- **Share more than just your job title** when meeting someone new. Share what makes you tick—something more memorable.

- **Admit where you have struggles or room for improvement** and that you're willing to roll up your sleeves and learn.

- **Highlight your differentiating factors**—what makes you qualified in some areas that may compensate for other gaps.

- **Have honest conversations with yourself and others** about gaps and learning opportunities when it comes to jobs.

Investment

- **Do the groundwork**—Step 1: *Know My Topic and My Contact* helps to prove your interest in an opportunity or partnership.

- **Share the research you've done** in advance of, and during, an interaction so your contact knows you're committed to the relationship.

- **Bring something to the table.** Take action, put in the work, and contribute ideas up front.

- **Combat "imposter syndrome"** by diving into research, and spend time learning a new area to boost expertise and gain confidence.

\ ' /

4

COMMONALITY

Commonality builds trust and opens the door

Can you relate to someone who has built a completely different career from you? Can two strangers build a relationship with each other, whether professional or otherwise? Can you partner with your competition? Can you have a mutually valuable meeting with someone who surpasses your experience by decades?

The answer is yes, yes, yes, and yes. How? Through The Knock Method Step 4: *Commonality*.

Commonality is the overlap between you and another person or organization. It's the shared interests, experiences, characteristics, or even beliefs that enable you to relate to one another and build trust. It makes strangers more familiar. Commonality helps you interact on the same level with others, regardless of professional expertise, industry, age, lifestyle, or title. (See Figure 4.1.)

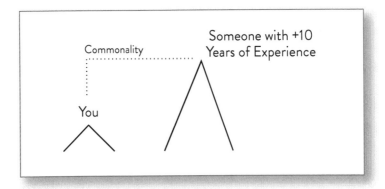

Figure 4.1—Commonality levels the playing field so you and your contact start from shared experience, regardless of how distant you start out from a career contact.

In a career context, you may share an alma mater, work within the same industry, have a similar experience switching careers, or embody a similar entrepreneurial spirit. Commonality narrows the gap between you and someone you've never met before to open the door to a conversation. And, once you've had an interaction, you can then keep filling your commonality cup as you build a long-term relationship—adding more areas of interest, experiences, values, accomplishments, projects, interactions, and even people in common. (See Figure 4.2.)

For example, I once met Dafna Michaelson Jenet, a Colorado state representative, through a nonprofit organization I was a part of, and I was inspired by her community work. Months later, I was on a call for that organization where she shared some of her experiences. I learned that she was an author and wrote a book about loss. I had experienced a similar loss and reached out to connect with her about this shared experience. After that phone call, I learned that she teaches a writing workshop, so I asked for more details about it, and I may sign up to be a part of it in the future. Our shared interests began to compound. This relationship began by having that first event in common, and as we had more interactions, we discovered additional commonalities like a

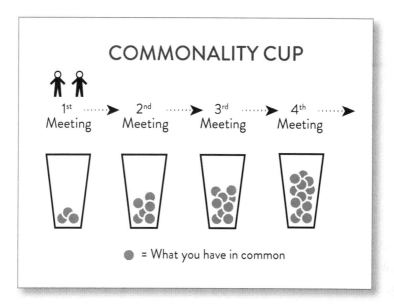

Figure 4.2—Fill your commonality cup as you add to your shared experiences with a contact in a long-term, mutually beneficial career relationship.

shared experience and an interest in writing, and we connected further over those. We now keep up with each other and interact on social media and personally through text, since we relate on topics ranging from personal to professional. It's not every day you get to connect personally with a state representative or politician, but commonality established trust early that opened the door to a conversation that led to more.

When someone says, go build your network, you might think, "Okay, but how?" Start with discovering commonality in professional interactions with contacts. While sharing something vulnerable about yourself and practicing authenticity (Step 3: *Own It*) can immediately help you connect with another person, having something in common enhances that feeling of connectedness.

Commonality helps us relate to and begin to understand others. It isn't just about what meets the eye. And it's not about being the same as someone else. It's about feeling connected to someone because of something you share, and sometimes it's something not apparent on the surface, as you'll learn in the next story.

FOR A SUCCESSFUL RESTAURATEUR, COMMONALITY RUNS DEEPER THAN A RESUME

Eric Silverstein followed his prescribed path and became a lawyer. From the outside, he fit in perfectly with his legal colleagues. The law firm where he worked, starting in 2007, employed a homogenous group, all well educated, sophisticated, and committed to defending the law. They all followed a similar path as Eric to get to their legal careers. But in his heart, Eric knew he didn't fit in. "I always felt like an anomaly," he said. "I was practicing law in Missouri, and I was the only Asian person there. I just didn't enjoy it that much and I thought, 'I don't know if I really want to be here.'" Even though he was doing what he had studied and worked hard to do, and he and everyone he worked with had obvious commonality in their career paths, he felt disconnected.

Plus, he felt a calling toward the hospitality industry in Austin. He was smitten with creative flavors, and inventive food is what he wanted to live and breathe.

So he did, and he still does.

More than ten years after leaving the legal industry, Eric has become the owner of a quintessential Austin restaurant group that includes The Peached Tortilla[1] restaurant, food truck, and catering business; Bar Peached, a bar-focused restaurant; and Peached Social House, an event venue. If you've traveled to Austin, you've probably seen his brand with the big peach or eaten in his airport restaurant (seriously! He has an airport restaurant!). His restaurants have been recognized by *Cosmopolitan*, Zagat, and *Forbes*. He appeared on *Live with Kelly and Michael*, was named one of *Plate* magazine's Chefs to Watch in 2014, and even published a cookbook featuring signature dishes and his family's cultures and flavors that I bought for my own kitchen.[2]

But you don't have a restaurant group and an airport eatery out of pure luck. Eric's success comes from a combination of tireless dedication to a dream, building quality relationships as he builds his business, and doing what he loves with people who share his passion—people with whom he has found the right mix of commonality. Eric has even gotten some press for building a friendship with one of his most direct competitors in the Austin restaurant community, because he saw past the competition and realized that what they had in common was much more powerful when they learned from each other than if they operated alone.[3]

Eric felt out of place in the legal industry, but he knew what kind of people he needed to be around in his future hospitality career. "I work best with people who appreciate hustling, don't mind working hard, love creating things, and respect each other, regardless of whatever background you come from," he said. He felt more insular and judgmental as a lawyer, but that was because he wasn't living his passion with people who shared it. Now, he's more open and connected.

When I met Eric in Austin in 2010, he had excitement in his eyes. I knew he had a passion that he was pursuing, but what I learned as we got to know each other better was how when he commits to something he feels is right in his core, he dedicates everything to making it happen. Once, after he had worked such long hours to operate his food truck, I suggested he eat more of his own creations because he looked exhausted. He was, but he powered through. He's someone who, at the end of what seems like the longest, hardest day, says, "That was a brutal day. But let's get up and face what comes our way tomorrow." He feeds off of this hustling, and even in the face of the COVID-19 pandemic, which put a gut-wrenching dent in the entire hospitality industry, he swerved as every new roadblock appeared. He had his restaurant patio sprayed with an antibacterial coating, he found ways to motivate staff and protect their well-being, and he reopened with fear, yet hope. It's all because he found his community who shares his commitment, determination, and unwavering love of hospitality. "Now, I speak Spanish; I have close relationships with my Hispanic workforce. My managers are from backgrounds totally different from mine, as are our servers and cooks." He found *his* kind of commonality, and relating to his team and extended network is what makes his business one of a kind.

Although his career and coworkers are now much more varied and diverse, culturally and in life experience, he believes he has found where he belongs, and he found the right kind of deep-rooted, productive, and effective commonality. He reflected on his team: "Our shared goal and belief is to provide the customer great service and best-in-class experience and food. We all like to create and grow. We all like to hustle, and we all want to do our best." He says that if somebody isn't on board with that, then they won't work on his team. "It's a shared belief in how we do business, and how we want to grow. We don't want to be stagnant. Our mentalities are aligned," he said with pride.

Eric explained that the rich commonality he shares with his team is what makes The Peached Tortilla special (along with the creative and flavorful dishes customers keep coming back for, of course). Because his whole team has this passion for service, next-level hospitality, and having an honest work ethic, it has served as a springboard for other businesses in Austin. One former employee started a taqueria that was named one of the country's top ten new restaurants; another started a breakfast food truck. A former chef started a catering company, a former catering manager started an exclusive dinner party business, and another former employee started a brand selling Thai-inspired sauce. "The Peached Tortilla is the hub of creation where people come first. They come here and to me to help vault them to the next level. I was on the other end of that sort of relationship in the beginning, needing a springboard that came in the form of connecting with people I shared common ground with," Eric said. It's that common ground that draws employees to work for The Peached Tortilla and that reinforces for Eric that he's living his professional dream. It's the right mix of like-mindedness that he was seeking in his former career that he knows with certainty he's found within his restaurant group, and which has led, in part, to his zesty success. And I can tell from our authentic, lasting friendship that has grown over the past decade, and from our interview—with the same excitement that was in his voice when we met ten years ago—that after his career change landed him among *his* kind of commonality, he's much happier and more fulfilled.

> "I was on the other end of that sort of relationship in the beginning, needing a springboard that came in the form of connecting with people I shared common ground with."
>
> —Eric Silverstein

HOW ERIC KNOCKS

Eric seeks out and attracts team members and individuals in his professional network who value quality service, creative hospitality, and dedication to working hard. He understands that commonality comes in many forms and that building relationships off of shared interests, beliefs, and goals, rather than lookalike backgrounds or career paths, is a recipe for success. He strives for higher quality, and that extends to his restaurants' brand, decor, food, and relationships that have made a significant impact on the Austin community in just a decade.

THE KNOCK METHOD STEP 4 IN ACTION

Commonality	Sought out his passion in hospitality and built relationships with staff and the community through shared values, work ethic, creativity, and quality customer service.

Many of the stories I've highlighted thus far in this book are about one-to-one relationships. But how groups of people find common ground when working together is just as important when it comes to career growth, economic progress, and making a difference in our world.

HOW THE ANTI-DEFAMATION LEAGUE FORMS UNLIKELY PARTNERSHIPS BASED ON COMMONALITY

Michael Lieberman has served for thirty years as Washington, DC, counsel for the Anti-Defamation League (ADL), an organization that does critical work to fight for equality and civil rights for all.[4] On many occasions over the years, he faced this challenge: The group must often work with people who disagree with some of its positions or policies. How does the ADL do it? It builds coalitions. This means it assembles representatives from various religious, social, and political groups and rallies around what they have in common to fight for a shared cause or policy.

For example, the ADL opposed the Catholic Church on just about every case concerning the Affordable Care Act (ACA). The

ADL supported employers funding the provision of contraception to employees, and the Catholic Church disagreed. But, as Michael said, "On immigration, the Catholic Church is one of ADL's best allies because it strongly supports anti-poverty initiatives." This collaboration works because they find commonality on some issues and work together on them.

The ADL fights for human rights and all kinds of equality issues, including gender, racial, and religious equality. The organization often takes positions opposing other organizations, or the president, or an important Senate leader, but it still finds a way to partner with them on other issues by focusing on what they have in common. "The advantage ADL has is they are not a single-issue organization," Michael explained. The ADL finds common interests among groups that may have very different ideologies and builds coalitions to fight for particular issues. "When we would ask a member of Congress, can you support us on this anti-bullying law, and they say no because they or their constituents don't want to support it, we won't burn the bridge. We will still go back to them and ask them to join a coalition on counterterrorism or immigration issues or pro-Israel issues." When coalitions come together, they get attention and amplify each other's voice, resulting in a bigger impact than the individual groups would have had separately.

This multi-issue orientation allows the ADL to ask for help frequently; even when turned away, they have another opportunity to go back to policymakers or decision influencers and ask if they can collaborate on a different cause—one that's of mutual interest. Michael told me that another way they are successful in promoting peace through policy is through the organization's twenty-five regional offices where ADL professionals partner with and advocate on behalf of local communities, policymakers, and their constituents. It's much easier for policymakers to relate to and put forth effort to advocate for an issue taking place on their own turf, one that's also important to the ADL. There's more in common and more at stake for their constituency.

HOW THE ANTI-DEFAMATION LEAGUE KNOCKS

The ADL's coalition work demonstrates that it's important to keep relationships going, even where there's disagreement, and to focus on long-term relationships to build on trust versus short-term, transactional asks. The ADL forms unique partnerships that garner support on important humanitarian issues by finding commonality, even among unlikely or dissimilar groups.

THE KNOCK METHOD STEP 4 IN ACTION

Commonality	Found common ground among groups when fighting for a cause, even if turned away on other issues.

COMMONALITY AND CAREER GROWTH: THIS STEP IN CONTEXT

The most familiar form of commonality that brings people together is knowing a person in common. And it works. It's no surprise that knowing an employee at a company who can recommend you to the hiring team—a job referral—is the top source of hiring, delivering more than 30 percent of overall hires in 2016.[5] Employers trust the recommendations of their employees and look to them to bring in top talent who may have things in common with their current workforce, such as similar experience or being a good fit with the culture. This is also why LinkedIn's second- and third-degree connections are so powerful—because no matter what company or person you look for on LinkedIn, you can attempt to find at least one person in common to make the world a bit smaller, allowing you to ask for an introduction from the person in common, or create an outreach message that feels less like a cold call and more productive for you and the recipient.[6]

Before you close this book, don't worry, I'm not going to give you that familiar "it's who you know" job search advice. In fact, you'll find the real value in building positive career relationships when it becomes less about how many people you know, or just knowing people enough to name-drop in an attempt to secure a job opportunity, and more about "how well do you know who you know?" High-quality, positive relationships matter for your community and for partnerships that lead to great things.

You know those people who seem to know everyone? Have you ever stopped to think, "How did they meet all those people in the first place, and how well do they really *know* all those people?" What steps did they take to meet and connect with people in a meaningful way, and where did these relationships begin? In this step of The Knock Method, you'll learn how to use the power of commonality in combination with the other steps to help you build new, quality relationships and nurture them over time so that your network is substantial and powerful.

Commonality is one place to start when you're meeting new people, whether you're going up to introduce yourself to someone at a company meeting on the suggestion of your manager, or you're reaching out to an author of an article that pertains to your work. It helps build trust out of the gate.

But beyond having common connections, there are other forms of commonality that bring professional relationships into being, including:

- **Geography/community:** When I started my own company, I found my first paying client, a career coach, because her office was in the same building as mine—our commonality was where we were geographically situated.

- **Shared interests/similar experiences:** I found one of my professional mentors when, after researching other experienced marketers at my company on LinkedIn, I discovered we both dedicated time to speaking and teaching at the university level.

- **Like-mindedness:** On the first day of working full time building my own company in 2011, I attended a networking event of fellow entrepreneurs. Others in my social sphere had expressed fear and concern about how I would make a living on my own after leaving a full-time job, but when I introduced myself and shared why I was there with this group, they clapped and congratulated me—they were people like me who had also struck out on their own.

When I was writing this book, I highlighted two to three things I had in common (my recommended formula) with every single person I reached out to for an interview. My response rate was nearly 100 percent—one person declined due to competing priorities at the time. Finding commonality was effective, especially since I applied it in combination with other steps in The Knock Method. If I hadn't met my prospective interviewees personally, I researched them and their work until I could find or create something in common. Sometimes that meant buying and reading their book (or downloading the preview on Kindle) or buying something at their store so I could reference their work and share my experience with it. Other times, it meant mentioning in my email an upcoming event they had in the city in which I lived, or expressing how much of a fan I was and supporter for their business or organization as a consumer or donor.

PRO TIP: Highlight two to three things you have in common with career contacts you're seeking to connect with.

Having something or someone in common with another person, team, or organization can give you a head start on a relationship, with a bit of trust already built into the foundation. Geographic locations, cities of residence, university or high school alma maters, former employers, travels, language fluencies, lifestyles, family makeup and role, hobbies, industries, or simply likes/dislikes including food, athletics, or movies can take a conversation forward, moving it from generic and easy to dismiss to worth prioritizing and opening the door to longer-term collaboration possibilities. Work to uncover commonality in your research before you connect, use it when you connect, then keep adding common experiences and shared interests to fuel your relationship in the long term.

COMMONALITY:
OPENING THE DOOR TO THIS STEP

THE KNOCK METHOD
Five steps to open doors and build relationships that matter

High-quality relationship: A mutually beneficial collaboration where both parties contribute and the outcome is stronger

Know my topic, my contact, and specifics up front. Prepare to connect.	**Research/Specifics**
Not about me. Focus on my contacts, us, and our mutual impact.	**Other-Centeredness/ Impact**
Own it. Be personal and authentic; invest in the relationship and the cause up front.	**Authenticity/ Investment**
Commonality. Build trust to open the door.	**Commonality**
Keep giving. Help others and practice generosity and gratitude.	**Generosity/ Gratitude**

Are there scientifically proven benefits to finding or incorporating commonality when building relationships? You bet.

When we find commonality with others, we trust them more, are more able to build rapport, and are more willing to collaborate. Research shows how and where commonality is applied and the impact it has on relationship building.

- **Identifying with others on a fundamental human level has a calming effect.** According to Rick Hanson, PhD, of the Greater Good Center at the University of California, Berkeley, when we think less about ourselves and more about how we're similar to other humans, "a wary tension in the body eases." He also says recognizing our common humanity allows us to "see others more clearly, be more effective with them, and feel less threatened."[7]

- **We're tribal by nature.** We trust people who have things in common with us because in early civilization, we stuck together in clans with similar cultures. As Fordham University professor Robert F. Hurley wrote in the *Harvard Business Review*, "At heart we are still quite tribal, which is why people tend to more easily trust those who appear similar to themselves."[8] This doesn't only apply to physical appearance—we trust those who we think are like us, think like us, behave like us, and value what we do. Working to uncover this is fascinating as career relationships unfold.

- **Commonality with others contributes to our innate desire for belonging, which makes us happy.** Belonging is a sense of sharing a common experience with others, and it affects our health positively. "A sense of belonging to a greater community improves your motivation, health, and happiness," said Karyn Hall, PhD, director/owner of the Dialectical Behavior Therapy Center in Houston, Texas.[9]

- **Commonality and similarity build rapport and quality relationships in retail settings.** People often have their guard up with salespeople, such as in a retail setting. But you might be more comfortable with and trust a store's salesperson if you find similarity or commonality with them, which builds rapport. According to marketing professors Dwayne Gremler and Kevin Gwinner in their journal article,

"Rapport-Building Behaviors Used by Retail Employees,"[10] "meaningful interactions" take place when a buyer and a seller share things in common during an interaction.[11] They also share research that shows that the more consumers think they have similarities with salespeople, the more likely they are to build rapport. And the more similar someone thinks they are to another person, the higher quality that relationship will be.[12]

- **Building rapport is a component of emotional intelligence, which helps us thoughtfully navigate relationships that feel good and connect with others.** In his *Harvard Business Review* article, "What Makes a Leader?" psychologist Daniel Goleman speaks to "common grounding," or discovering shared areas of interest with others as a key contributor to building rapport.[13] And he says social skills, which include relationship-building habits that establish rapport, are one of the five components of emotional intelligence. Goleman writes and speaks about several factors that lead to building rapport, one of which is that the relationship or interaction feels good—and that finding similarities with others feels good.[14]

In summary, when we discover commonality with others in a genuine way, we feel we belong, which makes us happy. We feel less threatened, which helps us to be more effective and see others more clearly. In partnerships, we trust more easily because we are tribal in nature, and we build rapport and a foundation for ongoing giving to each other.

HOW DO YOU DO IT?

While commonality often exists between people or groups, it can take some work to uncover it. But it's not enough to know about the things you have in common with someone. You have to bring that commonality to the surface in an interaction with someone to realize the value of being able to better relate to another. Here are three strategies you can use to uncover and establish commonality, and subsequently create meaningful and impactful experiences among individuals and groups:

First, think about how and when to use commonality based on each stage of an interaction—before, during, and after (see Figure 4.3).

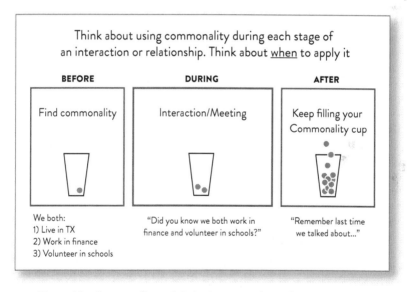

Figure 4.3—Commonality and timing in career relationship interactions.

Before: Find commonality

Before connecting with someone, research an individual or group—online, through social media, or by asking a mutual connection—to uncover information about them that overlaps with your background, interests, or goals. Sometimes, commonality is very specific, like you both went to the same high school; other times, when there's not much information available about someone, you may have to go a bit broader to find common qualities, like living in the same state and working in the same industry, just to get the ball rolling. The more points you have in common with someone, the easier it may be to reach out to them, craft your message, and converse, because you'll have a starting point for relating to them. I recommend looking for two or three things that you have in common with who you plan to reach out to as a way to build trust right away. The more you have in common, the more receptive they may be to you, even if they don't know you.

During: Use commonality

Once you uncover commonalities, use them in your communications, conversations, and introductions from others. Especially when you're meeting someone for the first time, bringing up commonality early can help you open the door and begin to establish rapport and trust, leading to a more productive conversation. Have fun with your commonality! Use it in an email subject

Especially when you're meeting someone for the first time, bringing up commonality early can help you open the door and begin to establish rapport and trust, leading to a more productive conversation.

line, ask a mutual friend to highlight it in an introduction, or share it as a photo from an event you both attended.

Here's an example that came into play for me when I was looking for a publisher for this book. On the recommendation of a colleague, I decided to reach out to the CEO of Greenleaf Book Group, the publishing company I interned with in college. I knew Tanya Hall, the CEO, was very busy and had existing clients and projects to prioritize, so I thought about how I could apply The Knock Method when reaching out to her so she'd be more receptive and responsive. I scoured through my old paper files from college (I probably should have gotten rid of them a long time ago), and lo and behold, found a handwritten thank-you letter on company letterhead given to me at the end of my internship—fifteen years prior. The fact that I had interned there was a major point of commonality that definitely broke the ice, resulting in an email reply. And she was amazed and excited to see the photo attachment of the letter. When I sought advice about publishing options, she offered to send me her book on the subject, so that after I read it, we could have a more productive conversation based in common ground, which led to this amazing opportunity—the book in your hand or on your device! When I visited the office for the first time, she mentioned the letter— it was a memorable detail that continues to make a big difference in why and how we work together.

After: Build commonality

The beauty of using the thoughtful steps in The Knock Method is that once you've opened the door to communication, you can nurture your relationships by adding commonalities you create together. Maybe you have an introductory phone call to share ideas and they suggest a book that may help you. After you read the book, you have a second interaction to follow up with what you've learned, leading you to connect more deeply, and maybe what you read gives you an idea for an article you think they'd enjoy. Then, the more involved your conversation and relationship becomes, the more you both have to share, and soon you're creating more commonality that strengthens the relationship, growing it into a longer-lasting one that's mutually beneficial. (Remember that commonality cup you're filling up?)

Next, treat commonality in professional relationships the same way you would in friendships. "Establish some sort of relationship, bring up commonality, or show that you understand what their business is. Mention previous things they talked about. Establish common ground," said Lifeway Foods CEO Julie Smolyansky, whose perspective I shared in Chapter 3.

As you and your contact build on your commonality, you may find yourself sharing more personal details with each other, and this may help your relationship blossom into a true friendship. Often, friendships are built on commonalities such as experiences, ideas, and communities.

"The transition from acquaintanceship to friendship is typically characterized by an increase in both the breadth and depth of self-disclosure," said University of Winnipeg sociologist Beverley Fehr, author of *Friendship Processes*. To keep the friendship going, according to author Karen Karbo in *Psychology Today*, that personal sharing needs to be reciprocal.[15] The more you share with each other, and the more authenticity you bring to the table from Step 3: *Own It*, the more opportunities you have to discover commonality and build on it. It has to be a conversation with both parties contributing for it to work and

> The more you share with each other, and the more authenticity you bring to the table . . . the more opportunities you have to discover commonality and build on it.

continue growing. If you notice you're reaching out over and over without much in return, or you feel like you're always asking the other person for something, don't forget to bring it back to Step 2: *Not About Me*. Focus on the other party and how you can help each other, and pair that with commonality to relate and feel connected.

Finally, build on what you have in common and what's going right, rather than initially focusing on problems or differences and trying to fix them. We should all be so lucky to have a treasured friend to turn to when we need advice, inspiration, a shoulder to lean on, a pun to laugh about, or an example of how commonality comes to life in academia. Samantha Becker is that to me. Beyond that, her impact on students and academic organizations globally is wildly innovative and far-reaching. She has published more than fifty NMC Horizon Reports, exploring the impact of technology on education, distributed to more than four million readers.[16] Yet, her craft is relatable and down-to-earth, and her charisma when she brings technology groups together in academia is equally magnetic. How does she do it?

As the executive director of creative and communications at Arizona State University's University Technology Office (UTO), Samantha says her organization uses appreciative inquiry to bring disparate groups together to unlock commonality and work toward common goals. According to the Center of Appreciative Inquiry, "Appreciative inquiry is a world view and a process for facilitating positive change in human systems, such as organizations and communities."[17] It works by building on what is working and what is positive within a group, rather than starting with what is broken or the current challenges a group faces. Samantha and her team have rallied the UTO, composed of more than ten groups and five hundred people, to establish a collaborative set of strategic goals for fiscal year 2021. "Universities, made up of so many units and organizations, are not famous for aligning around a central set of strategic goals," she said. "We use appreciative inquiry, scaffolding the collaborative process by building on strengths among individuals, then smaller groups, then the entire department. By finding common ground, we are doing something awesome—having north stars that we set for ourselves each fiscal year." In the past, she said, this type of strategic planning was set from the top down. But together with their executives, their vast team has come together around this collaborative process that works, and everyone's voices are heard and accounted for. And they don't stop by laying out those annual priorities. After workshops and live events full of interactive activities where different perspectives unite, the UTO shares out what it heard from the groups and invites them in for feedback and an internal quality assurance process. The end result is at least three checkpoints per year.

Samantha says after meeting individuals across teams one-on-one to hear their challenges and goals, it became clear that the teams were all facing the same challenges and going after the same things, but they were using different language and seeing the challenges through different lenses. What has led to this positive outcome where the varied groups are uniquely aligned? "We uncovered that the commonality is that we all want students to succeed. If you can break down walls and help people realize that's what we're all working towards, you can accomplish a lot." Samantha helped Arizona State University find the common thread: working toward the best possible student outcomes.

> **"We uncovered that the commonality is that we all want students to succeed. If you can break down walls and help people realize that's what we're all working towards, you can accomplish a lot."**
>
> —Samantha Becker

Remember *investment* from Step 3: *Own It*? The same way I ramp up expertise when I'm looking to invest in a cause or relationship and prove I'm dedicated to it, I spend time on Step 1: *Know My Topic and My Contact* using research to uncover and highlight commonality when building and nurturing career relationships. Sometimes it feels like a game and I get excited when I uncover what a contact and I already have in common—often before the first interaction.

If I identify someone on a team at work that I don't know but I'm looking to connect with, I search our internal organization chart and their internal online profile to read about them, their recent work, who they report to, and who's on their immediate team. I look for someone we have in common who can make an introduction or a team or project I can mention as a point of familiarity. I check LinkedIn to see what or who we may have in common.

One time I researched someone on LinkedIn prior to a phone call with them and found that we both worked for my first employer out of college. The company is no longer in business, so it was a rare connection—it broke the ice when I brought it up on the call.

Recently, I had the opportunity to help a prospective job candidate that I knew pursue a job at my company. They worked in the public sector/government technology field, so I thought about a man I knew at our company in the same industry and asked for his permission to make the introduction through email. When I connected them, I brought up their common industry so they could both get value from the conversation. I added a sentence at the end of my introduction email about how I started my career in government technology, just to make the connection among all of us more natural and relatable.

Again, I try to mention a minimum of two or three things in common to ease the unfamiliarity when communicating via email or phone with someone I don't know well.

Email Example Spotlight

Here's an email I sent to Jenna Benn Shersher, founder of Twist Out Cancer, whose story was highlighted in Chapter 3. Notice how I used commonality to create familiarity and relatability in the email. *Email is slightly edited for privacy and accuracy.*

February 12, 2019

Email Subject Line: Connecting + Book Interviews About TOC

Hi Jenna,

I hope all is well in Philly! If you recall, **I'm [name's] cousin, and a supporter of TOC/BWC, having attended Brushes in Chicago! [Commonality]** *It's so exciting to see your expansion into Austin and Chicago* **(two cities I've lived in that I still call home), [Commonality]** *and beyond! Not to mention your posts of [family member] are beyond adorable. My husband and I now live in Denver, but we keep our roots tight* **in Austin and Chicago. [Commonality]**

I'm reaching out because I'm writing a book about building strong relationships (networking) for career success. **Your global success building Twist Out Cancer is an inspiration, and you've undoubtedly needed to put yourself out there to connect with people you didn't know in cities across the world to communicate the TOC mission and garner support, event space, sponsors, and involvement. [Not About me, Other-Centeredness]** *Would you be up for a 15–30 minute interview in the next couple weeks to share how you've built relationships around the world to help further TOC's mission? I'm available most mornings before 10 a.m. EST, or afternoons/ evenings after 5 p.m. EST, and weekends are pretty flexible.*

The goal of my book (and related blog and workshops) is to build con-fidence for students and professionals by providing them with a formula for how to reach out to new people along their career path, as well as suc-cess stories of business leaders, nonprofit founders like yourself, [Impact]

and professionals who have built something from the ground up, building mutually beneficial relationships along the way.

What do you think?

Thanks,

Rebecca

Here's an email I sent to Julie Smolyansky, CEO of Lifeway Foods, whose advice is sprinkled throughout the book. I highlighted commonality and made it more personal by attaching a photo from her cookbook signing event that I attended as a reminder of who I was. *Email is slightly edited for privacy and accuracy.*

July 2018

Subject Line: Reconnecting + Career Success Interview

Hi Julie,

*I hope you are having a fantastic summer. I have been following along with **your success on Instagram since we met at your RPM blogger cookbook signing in April (see attached photo).** [Not About Me, Other-Centeredness, Specifics, Commonality, Investvent] Congratulations on your recent news segments and Entrepreneur article! [Research, Not About Me, Other-Centeredness] Also, I just tasted (and loved) the frozen kefir at Taste of Chicago last week! [Other-Centeredness, Not About Me, Commonality, Investment] As a blogger who loves to cook, entertain, and develop a healthy lifestyle, **I was excited to learn about kefir from you through the blogger event and have already incorporated it into our home kitchen.** [Investment, Not About Me, Other-Centeredness]*

*I'm reaching out, as **I've been very inspired to learn about your professional success with your family's business at Lifeway and your voice***

continued

to create positive change through Test400k and The Invisible War. [Not About Me, Other-Centeredness, Research, Specifics, Impact]

While I am a marketer by day, outside of work, I collect stories from successful professionals about how we all need help to get where we're going, and tips for building relationships where everybody wins (versus asking for help without giving too). For example, I have interviewed:

- *Adam Lowy, the founder of Move for Hunger, about how he founded his organization that mobilizes a fleet of moving trucks to pick up nonperishable food items from people who are relocating, and deliver them to local food banks.[18]*

- *Adam Grant, Wharton professor and New York Times best-selling author, about his approach to helping others, even when time is limited.*

I have incorporated these stories into a five-step method for building thriving career relationships, called The Knock Method, which I teach in workshops for students and professionals looking to navigate their own careers. (See photos from my recent workshop here.) **Throughout my career, I've noticed a gap in training, support, and mentorship when it comes to reaching out to role models, exploring new opportunities, and building a support network. These workshops, stories, and tools are my way of helping to bridge this gap. [Impact]**

While I know your time is valuable, **would you be willing to reconnect in person for 30 minutes–1 hour in the coming weeks for an interview to share some of your tips for building effective relationships as you build a successful business and create movements for change? I'd be excited and honored to share your stories on my blog and in upcoming workshops to inspire participants looking to create meaning in their own work. [Not About Me, Other-Centeredness, Giving, Generosity, Impact]**

I look forward to hearing from you,

Rebecca

Julie said she responded to my email because I mentioned coming to her cookbook event and that I enjoyed the book, and she thought, "She's taken some effort to establish a connection with me; I'm going to respond to her." She added: "You offered me something too, publicity, a write-up on the blog. You established a mutually beneficial opportunity to respond. *I had a reason to respond.*"

COMMONALITY: KEY TIPS TO APPLY THIS STEP

- **Share two or three commonalities in outreach emails or interactions** to be more relatable, open the door to a conversation, and build trust. Use your research from Step 1 to uncover commonality with others, and then use it in your interaction.

- **Don't forget to mention the commonalities that you uncovered** at the start of a message (email) or when it feels natural in a conversation. For example, when a prospective employer asks you in an interview to tell them a bit more about yourself, you can turn it back on them by mentioning something the two of you have in common (hello, other-centeredness).

- **Ask for an introduction** to someone from a mutual contact to start off with trust, and ask your common connection about that other person, to learn even more before chatting or meeting.

- **Go beyond mutual connections** when using commonality to establish rapport and trust. Take a look at their social media feeds, google them in case they are featured in news stories, and use LinkedIn or internal company directories to uncover other commonalities to bring to the forefront.

For example, seek out commonalities in a geographic location, city of residence, university alma mater or high school, former employers, travels, language fluency, lifestyle, family makeup and role, hobbies, industry, or simply likes/dislikes around food, athletics, or movies. These can take a conversation from generic and easy to dismiss to one worth prioritizing, and open the door to longer-term collaborative possibilities.

- **When someone reaches out to you, consider mentioning what the two of you have in common,** or mention something like "I had a similar experience" to make the conversation more natural, give the other person a bit of confidence, and ease any awkward tension since commonality can make people feel like they belong and feel good.

- **When bringing groups together, unlock commonality using appreciative inquiry.** Build on what individuals and groups have in common, what's going well, and what's positive, rather than starting with challenges and problem statements. The term itself makes me think of asking (inquiry) from a place of appreciation (appreciative). This helps establish common ground and a productive foundation for the interaction.

\ ' /

5

KEEP GIVING

Help others, and practice
generosity and gratitude

One Sunday morning, when I lived in Chicago in my late twenties, I was walking home quickly from an errand to get ready for a brunch event for bloggers. A twenty-something woman was in the middle of the street near a busy intersection, frantically trying to pick up a kitchen appliance—I think it was a juicer, and not a small one—and maneuver it back into the large box it had fallen out of. As someone who's no stranger to kitchen appliances and likes cooking at home, on instinct, I ran up to help her so we could get it in the box in record time and get out of the street before the traffic headed in our direction. She thanked me profusely, and we went our separate ways. I knew what she was going through; living in Chicago without a car meant I often found myself walking home with groceries or household items—one time, even new dishes (not advised). Sometimes I had to carry such a large or heavy haul that it covered my face and I could barely see where I was walking. It's a wonder I only had a grocery bag break on me once.

When I arrived at the brunch, coincidentally, the girl from the street was there! I took a double take. Yes, it was the same person. What are the odds? She was Sapna Dalal, the author of *The Vegetarian Tourist*,[1] a successful vegetarian-focused food and travel blog with a thriving community full of fun, humor, and adventure. She immediately introduced me to her friends, telling them about how I'd helped her earlier.

After that day, we became friendly, meeting once in a while or running into each other at restaurants, since we both had an interest in food. Sapna and I are still in touch today, and we support each other's work and stay up to date on our food and life adventures through social media and on the phone. We've even committed to being "accountability partners" for each other, making ourselves available for a boost of encouragement here or there or a brainstorming session related to our creative endeavors and career pursuits. (Consider an accountability partner as one kind of high-quality career relationship with high value—I highly recommend it).

While I barely gave any thought to helping Sapna in the street in the moment, this serendipitous meeting of two strangers highlights the residual positivity that comes from helping others in our path. I could have left her to fend for herself since I had somewhere to be. Instead, I helped lift the burden for someone else and made a friend in the process.

Step 5: *Keep Giving* in The Knock Method is different. The other four steps help you build and nurture relationships before and during interactions at a point in time, many of which are initiated by you. But Step 5 is ever present, addressing how to respond when others reach out to you, and how to keep adding value in your career relationships without needing a reason other than connecting with great humans. This step is continuously taking place, sparking relationships and keeping them going and growing beyond a single encounter or conversation.

The *keep giving* step is about the power of helping others while carving your own career path, and how putting energy into helping others and manifesting goodwill can advance everyone forward together. (I hope I'm still experiencing good karma from the day I met Sapna.) It's also about expressing gratitude, thanking those who take time to help you progress along your career. Finally, it's about following up and following through after connecting with individuals or organizations you're just getting to know. This step can make the difference between a single interaction of limited scope and an ongoing, mutually beneficial relationship.

How do relationships with giving embedded in them work? Let's take a look at how the prominent authors Adam Grant and Malcolm Gladwell met—and how they kept giving.

HOW GENEROSITY BUILT A RELATIONSHIP BETWEEN A BUDDING AUTHOR AND AN ALREADY INFLUENTIAL ONE

When Adam Grant was in grad school at the University of Michigan in 2005, Malcolm Gladwell, one of *Time*'s top 100 influential people, was on a book tour for his newly released book, *Blink*,[2] and would be stopping at the university's bookstore. One of Adam's classmates, Dan Gruber, emailed Malcolm ahead of his trip and mentioned that their group of social science and management PhD students, including Adam, was interested in meeting him for a meal when he was in town, given their common interest in getting academic ideas out into the world. Malcolm accepted. "I was stunned that this mega-successful author was willing to give his time to a group of strangers starving their way through grad school," Adam said.

After that dinner, Adam became excited about the prospect of spending more time with Malcolm, but didn't have a good reason to ask him for more of his time. Adam didn't want to be a "Taker." A Taker, in Adam's terminology, is someone who takes from others more than they give of themselves. Years later, as Adam was writing his first book, *Give and Take*,[3] he referenced Malcolm's thinking.

Once his book was completed, it was suggested that Adam send Malcolm a prerelease copy of *Give and Take* to ask him for an endorsement, but Adam didn't feel comfortable reaching out. Instead, he reached out to ask if he could come say hi when Malcolm was in town to give a talk, even though it had been almost ten years since they had met.

Before the talk, Adam reintroduced himself and walked with Malcolm to meet with a group of students. Finally, just before Malcolm left the university, Adam left him a copy of his book with a note thanking him for his generosity in meeting with him and his classmates years ago, and with the students during this visit. He noted in the inscription that Malcolm exemplified what Adam wanted to convey in his book about "Givers"—those who give more than they take in relationships. This was a more personal and more meaningful gesture than just sending a book and requesting a blurb, as many authors do. A few months later, in a *New York Times* article, Malcolm cited Adam as one of his favorite social science writers.

Their work together was just beginning. In 2012, Adam created the Authors@Wharton speaker series. When Malcolm's book *David and Goliath* launched, Adam reached out to the publisher, offering to host Malcolm on his book tour and buy hundreds of books to give away to students. The publisher replied, "Malcolm Gladwell will contact you directly." They arranged a date for his visit, and Adam got to interview Malcolm during the event for about a thousand people.

"This was a wonderful opportunity to exchange ideas and get

to know him a little better," Adam said. "Afterwards, he kindly offered advice on my work going forward." Adam continued to give to the relationship in his LinkedIn post, explaining what went on behind the scenes of *David and Goliath* and what makes Malcolm Gladwell an intriguing writer.[4]

About their meetings after that first one, Adam said, "I never asked; I tried to create opportunities for him to have a bigger impact." The result was getting to know each other on an ongoing basis. Adam Grant and Malcolm Gladwell have now collaborated on a multitude of projects, including live events and podcasts, garnering significant mindshare, and their collective intellect has reached and inspired global audiences.

HOW ADAM KNOCKS

Adam didn't lead with an ask. He established a relationship, built rapport, and created opportunities for others to shine. He behaves in a way that elevates others' work, and that creates new, unexpected opportunities for him. Adam created an opportunity for Malcolm Gladwell to share his research, knowledge, and work with students during each interaction. Even when Adam shared his own book, *Give and Take*, he didn't ask for anything in return, but instead practiced gratitude and gave it as a gift without any expectation. Adam continues to give, contributing to the relationship with Malcolm, writing articles about his work, and interviewing him on his podcast. As a result, their collection of interactions has grown into a thoughtful and inspiring collaboration. They now have an ongoing long-term relationship where they give to each other, and the result is more impactful and fun for their larger joint audience.

THE KNOCK METHOD STEP 5 IN ACTION

Keep Giving (Generosity)	Created opportunities to elevate Malcolm Gladwell's exposure and impact among students and broader audiences. Approached the relationship from a point of contribution and collaboration, rather than for self-serving needs.
Keep Giving (Gratitude)	Expressed gratitude, with a handwritten note, and generosity before, during, and after each interaction.

KEEP GIVING: THIS STEP IN CONTEXT

How can it be that giving your own time, resources, and energy can help you progress when that time and those resources are limited? Your natural instinct might be to think that if you give others your time, you may not have time to work on your own projects. Or that if you invest in other businesses, you may not be able to maintain your own business profits. Or that if you take vacation or time away from work, you can't possibly grow your career because you're not spending time fueling it. Far from it. According to Alex Soojung-Kim Pang, author of *Rest: Why You Get More Done When You Work Less*, "When we treat rest as work's equal partner, recognize it as a playground for the creative mind and a springboard for new ideas, and learn ways to take rest more effectively, we elevate it into something valuable that can help calm our days, organize our lives, give us more time, and help us achieve more while working less."[5] It may also seem backward that to invest in others is to invest in yourself. Entrepreneur, investor, and former CEO Amy Rees Anderson observes that putting others first can be intimidating, "because in the moment it feels so counterintuitive to put others' needs above your own,"[6] especially when doing that means you must set aside your own pursuits.

When we were kids, we learned that what goes around comes around, that mistreating others or speaking poorly about others may come back to us later in the form of a bad reputation, closed doors on opportunities, or bad karma. The same holds true for good karma. Whether you believe in karma or not, giving and helping others *will* help you progress further than if you constantly take from others for your own progress.

I learned this myself. When I set out to write *Knock* six years ago, the book's focus was narrow and shallow, representing the self-centered kind of individualism that I now know can be harmful and short-sighted. I sought to answer: *How do we ask for help from others in pursuit of our career goals?*

But a lot of learning can take place in six years. During that time, I expanded my professional experience helping multiple large clients and navigating the large organization I'm a part of. I dove into social psychology research topics like other-centeredness, prosociality (helping other people), commonality, and authenticity. I interviewed successful professional leaders whose interpersonal relationships fueled their accomplishments.

I learned volumes, and as a result, *Knock* encompasses so much more than simply "asking for help" for yourself. For example, the original idea for Step 5 in The Knock Method was about reputation. Now, with the evidence and experience I've gained leading to a broader and more productive and progressive view, this step is about generosity, giving, and gratitude, acknowledging the good that emanates from others and propels us all.

Recall how when Jenna Benn Shersher of Twist Out Cancer asks for support for her organization, she highlights how fundraising dollars impact a global community, and her community supporters then rally around the organization's mission.

Meaningful partnerships emerge when we focus on how we can make a difference for other people, groups, organizations, and communities—together.

When Jane Dutton, coauthor of *Awakening Compassion at Work*, and I first talked about The Knock Method, she illuminated the wider impact my five-step approach can make on our networks and our world, based on her career of research, writing, and teaching about similar topics. Instead of taking from other people and relationships, or having a self-focused view of one's reputation, The Knock Method is about propelling personal energy forward, giving, helping, and being generous to others. It's also about seeing that interpersonal competition isn't the optimal way to develop yourself and your career, and that gratitude and generosity have a ripple effect. While it's reasonable and necessary that we focus on our careers to pursue our passions, make a living, and live our own lives, if we expand our view to think about what would happen if we all helped others more in the process, we can make a more positive impact on those around us.

Instead of taking from other people and relationships, or having a self-focused view of one's reputation, The Knock Method is about propelling personal energy forward, giving, helping, and being generous to others. It's also about seeing that interpersonal competition isn't the way to progress, and that gratitude and generosity have a ripple effect.

Thinking beyond our own personal impact, giving to others, practicing gratitude, and spreading kindness result in a positive reputation, but one generated by others. We don't define it ourselves, nor can we chase it. If you practice giving to others as you progress, you won't be so concerned with the natural reputation you've built because you'll be more excited to help another person.

Consider the COVID-19 pandemic, which was taking place as I was writing this chapter. At first, many of us started out considering wearing a mask to protect ourselves. Then, as more research surfaced that the virus was more contagious than initially thought, we learned that wearing a mask could protect those around us, especially if we were silent carriers. Taking actions to protect the health of our greater community and our world became so important that we were ordered to stay home, almost eliminate normal activities, and close businesses. We learned that our collective actions—or lack thereof—to "shelter in place," wear masks, and focus on cleaning our environments and shared spaces had a hand in how quickly the disease was contained or spread. We had the power to protect others just as much as ourselves. And we began to see that our individual actions could contribute to the collective good to prevent further strain on our health-care system, possibly giving those working on treatment more time to improve it and strategies to address this global challenge.

If we all think more broadly and focus on building quality, mutually beneficial relationships in our careers, everyone will realize more success and progress a bit further.

The same goes for taking actions, small and large, to help others around us, including in our careers. If we all think more broadly and focus on building quality, mutually beneficial relationships in our careers, everyone will realize more success and progress a bit further. And when we're all more successful, we tackle more challenges, find new solutions, make new ideas come to life, and cultivate more positive shared experiences.

Jane Dutton addresses this bigger picture. "This really matters," she said. "It's so beyond firms or individuals performing well. We are in so much trouble—whether with our environment or inequality, we don't have enough money to fix it. What will fix it is unleashing human potentiality in humans [through] meaningful human connection that strengthens and lifts people up."

Barbara Fredrickson, a psychology professor at the University of North Carolina, summarizes the power of giving this way: "By creating chains of events that carry positive meaning for others, positive emotions can trigger upward spirals that transform communities into more cohesive, moral, and harmonious social organizations."[7] As you build your career, think about how helping others and having an other-centered mindset along the way can encourage others—at any stage in their career—to generate positive relationships, emanating outward to create a lasting impact on social circles, workplaces, and communities.

KEEP GIVING: OPENING THE DOOR TO THIS STEP

There are many ways to give and assist others in career relationships beyond helping someone get a job or make a sale.

THE KNOCK METHOD
Five steps to open doors and build relationships that matter

High-quality relationship: A mutually beneficial collaboration where both parties contribute and the outcome is stronger

Know my topic, my contact, and specifics up front. Prepare to connect.	**Research/Specifics**
Not about me. Focus on my contacts, us, and our mutual impact.	**Other-Centeredness/ Impact**
Own it. Be personal and authentic; invest in the relationship and the cause up front.	**Authenticity/ Investment**
Commonality. Build trust to open the door.	**Commonality**
Keep giving. Help others and practice generosity and gratitude.	**Generosity/ Gratitude**

Let's dive into two forms of giving in professional relationships that help us truly connect on an intimate, human level with other individuals—giving that has truly transformative effects.

MENTORING AS A WAY TO GIVE

Mentoring others is a way you can keep giving to and for others. Mentoring is a unique kind of help—one that's consistent, trusted, neutral, and supportive. When it's effective, it can have a powerful, positive impact on the lives of both the person being mentored and the mentor.

In the chapter "How Do You Feel When You Knock?" I highlighted research that said people have a natural desire to belong and feel connected to others,[8] and that people are often caught between wanting to belong, yet wanting to feel independent.[9] Tammy D. Allen from the University of South Florida and Lillian T. Eby from the University of Georgia connect that human desire to belong to mentorship.[10] Their research proves that an effective mentoring relationship is one where those being mentored feel they belong through connectedness to another person in this unique type of positive relationship. For example, you might have an effective mentor relationship if you feel your mentor is a trusted champion in your corner, you are connected to them consistently over time, and you feel accepted by them. Allen and Eby say that a feeling of belonging and acceptance "makes mentoring relationships a powerful agent for individual growth and well-being."[11] Their research suggests that mentoring others effectively, in which there is a sense of belonging, makes a tangible difference for those being mentored by improving their life satisfaction, self-esteem, school involvement and performance, and career outcomes.

A feeling of belonging and acceptance "makes mentoring relationships a powerful agent for individual growth and well-being."
—Tammy D. Allen and Lillian T. Eby

After learning from this research, I can attest to the power of this feeling of belonging. There's something very comforting about the professional relationship I have with my own mentor, Adam H. We've met on video calls monthly for about three years, and I recently had the opportunity to meet him in person. I feel I can trust him because he has an objective perspective, one that helps me better advocate for myself. He stands up for me, even when I doubt myself in professional and work situations. As a result, I feel less isolated and more confident, which contributes to my well-being. And he brings ideas to me that I wouldn't otherwise get from friends, family, or my manager, because my mentor has an interest in sharing his experiences with me and shows care and compassion without distractions like company hierarchy, competition, or personal bias. I practice some of the approaches he's taken with me with emerging female professionals I have the privilege to mentor. I hope to model this unique kind of friendship, which I intend to develop long term with those I get the opportunity to help as they develop their own professional lives.

The one being mentored decides whether a mentoring relationship is effective and has a positive impact on their life, but the responsibility falls on both people in the relationship, maybe even a bit more on the mentor to make it successful.

We know mentoring works, and it's tied to positive career outcomes for those being mentored. But what makes it difficult to get mentoring right? How do you, as a mentor, help others grow and develop their careers? The one being mentored decides whether a mentoring relationship is effective and has a positive impact on their life, but the responsibility falls on both people in the relationship, maybe even a bit more on the mentor to make it successful.

Gerald Chertavian is the founder of Year Up,[12] an impactful organization that is closing the Opportunity Divide by empowering young adults to move from minimum wage to meaningful careers. Year Up serves talented and motivated young adults who are disconnected from the economic mainstream by ensuring that they gain the skills, experiences, and support necessary to thrive in professional careers. Over the course of a year, students complete coursework for college credits and earn a six-month internship at a partner company—all while connecting with local mentors and business leaders. In being connected to opportunity, these young adults are able to launch professional careers, strengthen their communities, and lift others while they climb.

I am so grateful to have served as a mentor for a Year Up program participant through her graduation and remain a dedicated supporter of their program. In supporting Stef, the student I mentored, whether it was hearing how she juggled school and work responsibilities, listening to her share an accomplishment from her internship, or simply being a safe place to share what was on her mind on a given day, I learned from her life experiences and how to keep giving to our mentoring relationship. When I attended her Year Up graduation, I had chills and watched, full of pride, as she was handed her diploma, knowing that whatever she did next would be backed by a network of supporters through the organization, including me.

Since its founding in 2000, Year Up has served more than thirty thousand young adults and matched over nine thousand formal mentorships. In addition to the mentor program, every student is matched with a coach who serves in a mentor-like role throughout their Year Up experience—as well as working with internship supervisors, guest speakers, and other volunteers who provide support. Gerald explained: "Nothing is more important in the development of a young person than a positive, consistent adult in their lives."

Many of Year Up's program participants don't get this type of support from parents or family members. According to Gerald,

"Mentoring provides a great deal of value to learn, grow, solve problems, be a listener. Someone who is able and willing to make that connection in a consistent fashion is incredibly helpful." But mentoring is hard to get right. Even at Big Brothers Big Sisters of America, the most effective mentor-matching organization in the country, "Research into Big Brothers Big Sisters community-based program practices has found that as many as one in five matches end before six months, with only 45% lasting for the full 12 month intended duration."[13] Why did the other 55 percent end early? Mentors misconstrue the fact that the mentee may not know how to grasp the hand the mentor is extending, and so the mentor feels the mentee doesn't like or want them. "True mentoring is not something you do because you want to get something out of it," Gerald said. "You're committed to the act. It requires people to make a commitment and check egos and selves at the door when going into the mentoring relationship. It's not about you. It's about the person you are trying to support."

If you find yourself with the opportunity to mentor someone, consider it a privilege—a personally and professionally enriching opportunity to support their career development. You will both undoubtedly learn and grow from the experience, but consider the commitment you're making. If you sense hesitation on the part of the person you're mentoring, that is an opportunity to build trust and consistency, and provide them with the feeling that they belong and that you are their advocate. Think about other-centeredness and how to give to them over time for the simple purpose of nurturing them to fuel their career progress. Be someone for them to lean on as they navigate life challenges and opportunities.

"True mentoring . . . requires people to make a commitment and check egos and selves at the door when going into the mentoring relationship. It's not about you. It's about the person you are trying to support."

—Gerald Chertavian

BE COMPASSIONATE IN YOUR CAREER

When it comes to building quality relationships in our careers, compassion is an essential way to give to others. In *Awakening Compassion at Work*, Jane Dutton and Monica C. Worline define compassion as "more than an emotion; it is a felt and enacted desire to alleviate suffering."[14] They describe a thought experiment in which information is shared within a company about an employee's family losing their home in a fire. An organization that is positive, nurturing, and empowering for its employees feels empathy and may take actions to do something to help. An organization with a more competitive, high-pressure culture may read the email in their busy inbox but go about their day to tackle other pressing challenges. Even though the individuals in this work environment may be compassionate, the systems and culture may guide their less-than-attentive response to a tragedy affecting a coworker.

Why even consider compassion in the workplace? Dutton and Worline believe it's because we spend a lot of time in these places, and as a result, they shape us as individuals. Plus, the companies and organizations we work for may have more robust and coordinated resources to help the employees who are so crucial to their operation.

In my experience, places of work and professional organizations are made up of individuals who experience love, loss, and adversity, and have unique interests, all of which shape who they are when they go to work. So, why should the workplace *not* support and help employees when they need it? The phrase, "It's not personal; it's business," no longer applies. Business *is* personal, and we should take the human aspect of it into consideration.

> **The phrase, "It's not personal; it's business," no longer applies. Business *is* personal, and we should take the human aspect of it into consideration.**

If compassion is about a response to someone's suffering—such as a personal loss, illness, or hardship—then a compassionate workplace must enable its employees to feel comfortable opening up when they are suffering. "Psychological safety" is a social psychology term that pertains to group settings like the workplace, and it means that a group's members "share the belief that they will not be threatened personally or socially by exposing their self, identity, status, or standing when engaging in learning behaviours such as asking for help, seeking feedback, admitting errors or lack of knowledge, trying something new or voicing work-related dissenting views."[15] When building relationships with coworkers, it's critical that you feel safe to be vulnerable when you are suffering, that your career won't be disrupted or your growth penalized, and that you'll be met with acceptance, empathy, and compassion. It's equally important that you show compassion if those you work with are going through a hard time. As Jenna Benn Shersher of Twist Out Cancer said, "Bring your guard down, and others will." The more you share, the better others can help you, even at work.

Does compassion really matter in our work? Will it cause us to lose focus on shareholders, profits, bad reviews from customers, competition, or even weathering a pandemic? According to the team of Jane Dutton, Sara Rynes, Jean Bartunek, and Joshua Margolis in their journal article, "Care and Compassion Through an Organizational Lens: Opening Up New Possibilities," we must see the bigger picture that work shapes our world and that how we treat each other at work matters for our humanity. In writing about the compassion organizations should strive to have, they state: "Rather than assuming that revenues, profits, and wages or salaries are the ultimate (and, often, sole) objectives of organizations and organizing, attention would be focused additionally or instead on the health, happiness, well-being, and sustainability of organizations, their members, and those they serve."[16]

They added, "When seeking to build high-performing organizations that meet the challenges of a twenty-first century work environment, compassion matters more than most people recognize."[17] It results in higher levels of workforce productivity, effectiveness, and employee and customer loyalty and productivity.[18] Employees in a compassionate workplace who feel accepted as they are may be more inclined to refer potential candidates for openings to attract top talent, for example, helping the company better compete in the marketplace. Compassionate workplaces are better for our well-being because employees feel safe to be who they are, ask for help, or share a personal tragedy.

While I was writing this chapter, my husband and I faced a personal tragedy. We experienced a complication in the second trimester of our pregnancy, resulting in surgery and the loss of our child. Time stopped for us. I didn't know how to cope, how to work, or how to conduct my daily life since our world was turned upside down. The surgery was unexpected, and the physical impact to my own health was unpredictable.

I immediately shared what was taking place with my manager at work, asking him to keep it confidential among our team. I was vulnerable and unsure how he would respond. I didn't even know what to ask for or what I needed and barely got the words out. He responded with more generosity and compassion than I could have ever imagined. He told me to log off of my computer and just go—to care for myself and my husband, and grieve. We checked in with each other again the next week. Over time, and following company guidelines for time off, we came up with a plan for me to take bereavement time and to determine the right time for me to come back to work, when I could be present and approach work with a clearer mind.

My manager knew me well enough to know that I would feel like I needed to be at work shortly after our loss, but he encouraged me to dedicate time to focus on healing. He knew I would make up for lost time with extra effort in the future, although that didn't even come up in our conversation. He knew that diving back into work right away and not focusing on myself wouldn't be healthy for me or helpful for my colleagues, team, and company.

I am overwhelmed with gratitude for the compassion he and our leadership graced me with during my biggest heartache and most serious surgery. It is amazing how our lives, our work, and our relationships are enriched when we strip away our to-do lists, our routines, and our work pressures and simply connect on a human level. Of course, my manager and my team members stepped in to fill in for me while I was out, as I would do for my teammates. I expressed my gratitude to my manager with a personal gift and note, even though nothing would be enough.

During my time off, feelings of guilt started to creep in because I felt I should be working like everyone else, especially since this took place during the height of the pandemic. But then I realized everyone has times of need. We all need help to get where we're going, and giving support and showing compassion to others in times of suffering is one significant behavior that really makes a difference when building high-quality connections, at work and otherwise.

HOW DO YOU DO IT?

To help others better, you need to know more about them. But it starts with you. You can model authenticity, from Step 3: *Own It*, and project openness. If you ask questions to get to know someone better and share something personal about yourself, you'll inspire others to do the same. The more people in your network who open up to each other, the easier it will become to give and be helpful.

This is where we all have a shared responsibility to apply the rest of The Knock Method steps to interactions with our contacts—so that they can better understand who we are and how we can help each other.

It helps when others thoughtfully connect with us so that we don't have to go back and forth on email before getting the facts. For example, if a colleague conducts research (Step 1: *Know My Topic and My Contact*) to learn your location and time zone before proposing a few times to meet, they will have made it easier for you to respond and make time to help. Or if they use authenticity (Step 3: *Own It*) to share that they're new to the business world, having just graduated from college, you may be able to provide them with resources that are more helpful, given their level of experience.

On the flip side, if someone reaches out and you don't have enough detail to determine if or how you can help, ask a few key questions to understand their goals. Then if you aren't the best person to help, you can point them to a resource or person who could provide better help.

Adam Grant mentions redirecting requests, rather than being a dead end, as one of his best ways of helping others.

How does he help others despite his limited time, resources, availability, and other priorities, especially after the flood of requests that followed the popularity of his book about connecting with people? "When *The New York Times* tells people you like helping strangers and rarely say no, this creates an interesting dilemma," he explained. "If someone wanted marketing advice on a business plan, I'm not a marketing professor or an entrepreneur. I've never started a business so I'm not an expert on any of these topics, so I'd recommend books or people they might contact." He feels that by redirecting them to helpful resources and not trying to help with every request, he will help people learn to research so they can figure out how to more effectively reach out next time to those who may have more relevant experience.

I've wondered how not to come off as stingy or unresponsive yet protect my time, and what to do when my experience doesn't lend itself to a specific request. Like me, you might wonder how to prioritize who to respond to and who to help, especially when you don't have an answer. As Adam explained, "You have to prioritize who, how, and when you will help." He follows the habits of the most aspiring Givers that he's met. Adam asks himself several questions:

- **Who and how can I help?** He prioritizes those he can help and those he wants to help. He helps family first, students second since he's a professor, colleagues third, then everyone else fourth. I fell in the fourth category when Adam responded to my email, declining my invitation for an in-person interview when he was traveling to Chicago, but offering an alternative—a calendar tool he uses where I could select a time for a phone call. (See the Email Example Spotlight on page 211.)

  He also considers whether saying yes to helping with one request will jeopardize his ability to help in an area of higher importance.

Last, he thinks about whether he can help uniquely. "If someone asks for something that is not my core expertise, will I be inefficient or do a disservice to myself and to them by trying to expend time and energy to learn it?" If he's not knowledgeable on the topic, he outsources the request and redirects when possible to resources or others who may be better able to help. In fact, Adam did this when I reached back out years later to share the impact of our interview, explaining that, at the time, it had helped more than twenty-five students and young professionals (hey, you have to start somewhere). He then replied and referred me to one of his researchers to continue the conversation, which led to my interview and ongoing professional relationship with Jane Dutton.

- **How much of an impact can I make?** Consider the impact you will make on others. Adam considers whether the person seems to be a Giver (someone who gives more than they take in relationships), a Matcher (someone who matches the level of giving in a relationship), or a Taker (someone who takes more than they give). Do they have a plan for how they're going to take what he provides—money or time or advice—and use it to help other people? In other words, what meaningful impact will helping have?

- **Has the other person made an investment in the potential relationship? How applicable and tailored is this request to me, my work, and the impact I'm trying to make?** He pays attention to the other person's preparation, as I described in the investment element of Step 3: *Own It*. Have they done their homework, asked in a respectful way, and tailored their outreach to something he's excited about and able to offer?

Adam's process doesn't just ensure that he's helping people to the best of his ability and in a way that matters. By prioritizing and having a system in place for how to best help others, Adam is also helping optimize his time so he can continue to do the work that attracted people to him in the first place. According to Ron Carucci in the *Harvard Business Review*, "The greatest helpers set clear expectations from the outset."[19] As a consultant and executive coach—where his job is to help others—Carucci said that one of the first boundaries he sets with clients is that he will never care about their success more than they do. This means that the person needing help needs to put in the work (remember *investment* from Step 3: *Own It?*), and the helper's job isn't to swoop in and do the work for the other person. The helper's role is to enable them, point them in the right direction, give them resources or connections to follow up on, and help them get further than they are today.

To help others effectively, some prep work needs to happen, often by the one asking for help. Remember that famous quote from *Jerry Maguire*, "Help me help you"? Others need to help you help them—both parties must make an effort so that help given is appropriate for the situation, and effective.

I often receive messages on LinkedIn from people I've met throughout my career, mentioning their interest in applying for a job at a company I have a connection to and attaching their resume before we have a conversation. While I may not be in a hiring position, I want to find the best way to help people in my network follow their passions and pursue their career goals. However, it is presumptuous to assume I'd simply take resumes and pass them on to others without having a two-way conversation. Here's why:

- **We should catch up first.** For one, the asker needs to put in the work to share why they're reaching out to me in particular, and why their experience might be a fit for the job. They might want to ask some questions to see if I know a particular connection well enough to make an introduction, or if I'm the best person to talk to about the opportunity.

- **I need to prepare and feel prepared to recommend someone.** As the person in a potential helping position, I'm not prepared to recommend someone I've met only once or twice, or worked with years prior, simply based on a quick message and a resume.

- **I need to consider how I will be perceived in my network.** I'm committed to making sure any referral I make is worth the time for those that I'm asking for help from on the job seeker's behalf. I hold my relationships close and at a high standard so that my community knows that when I send someone their way, I've qualified that person's experience and character, my referrals can be trusted, and I am assured they will follow through.

- **I want others to open the door to a conversation so I can understand how we can help each other, rather than replying to a one-sided request.** It may turn out that I'm not too familiar with the company they're applying to, or I met a contact at that company in my network one time many years ago, so reaching out to refer someone for a job may not be the most helpful. Through a conversation, I may think of someone who's closer to the company or role that could be an even bigger help, but we wouldn't know that from a one-way message with a resume attached. I believe the person making the request should open the door to a conversation in which we can reconnect and get to know each other's current work, and even share what's new in our lives, instead of jumping out of the gate with an ask. Sound familiar? This is what The Knock Method is all about—creating positive career relationships where both parties give and the outcome is stronger and longer lasting.

WHAT TO DO IF YOU'RE JUST STARTING YOUR CAREER OR ARE NEW TO AN INDUSTRY OR ROLE

If you're starting out, either in your career or a new job opportunity, you may be wondering where to begin and what you have to offer that will help other people. It's a common misconception that if you're less experienced in your career, you may not have something to offer an individual who has decades of experience. Bring out that confidence from Step 3: *Own It*! Even if you're just starting out, you always have something to give.

Here are three steps to discover your power to help others:

1. **Draw from your life experience.** Have you moved multiple times and lived in several states? It's likely you have some strategies you can share for how to adjust to a new environment, job, or company. Have you endured some uncertainty or even lost a job due to an economic downturn or a company's financial struggles? You likely have some ways you coped, and others can benefit from what you learned along the way.

2. **Draw from your natural strengths.** If your friends and family always confide in you when they have personal challenges, your trustworthiness can be an asset to new people in your orbit. If you've gotten compliments on your resume format

in the job search, helping others refine their resumes might be a way to help. If you have endurance and have run a marathon or participated in athletics that require discipline, you can offer comfort to someone who's in the midst of a long job search.

3. **Be curious and listen.** Read your favorite news sources. Subscribe to industry research, newsletters, and podcasts. Take advantage of company learning opportunities or local training programs for skills you're interested in. Then, listen with dedicated attention to your friends, colleagues, and those around you, whether in person, on the phone, or on social media. Pay attention to what answers others are seeking. You might be someone who can help them find the answers. You'll likely be able to offer knowledge, information, and resources you've come across that can help them.

What if you're often on the giving end of relationships and receive frequent career requests? Jessica Malkin, former CEO of Chicago Ideas, believes in sparking connections and nurturing many relationships through giving. "Let's say for years and years, you're more on the giving end of trying to help everyone else do their thing. I think there are dark days or opportunity days when I need to go to the eATM [emotional bank] and get some cash out," she said. She taps the people in her life informally, considering them her personal board of directors when she needs something and doesn't know where to go for help. One day when she's in need, she'll be the one receiving help like she's offered up to other people through her commitment to connecting with and helping others. Being in a constant state of giving cultivates a more fruitful network for all of its members, creating a resource that's there when she needs it.

Email Example Spotlight

Earlier in this chapter, I mentioned that when I reached out to Adam Grant, he declined my invitation for an in-person interview, but offered an online calendar to select a time for a phone call instead. He was able to give his time and expertise, only in a different way from I had asked for. See the alternative he provided highlighted. *Email is slightly edited for privacy and accuracy.*

Hi Rebecca,

Thanks for writing—I'm honored that you're reading my book, let alone enjoying it. [Gratitude, Investment, Authenticity]

Congratulations on taking the plunge to write your first book. It's a whirlwind trip to Chicago, and my schedule is jam-packed, but I'm happy to chat by phone. Feel free to sign up for a time here: https://www.time-trade.com/book/00000 [Giving, Generosity]

Cheers,

Adam

KEEP GIVING: KEY TIPS TO APPLY THIS STEP

Helping others in professional settings has become a normal part of my week, and I love being able to help others solve a problem, get further along on their career path, conduct research to help them gain clarity, and pursue their passion. That's why I wrote a book about it. When I connect one of my contacts to another, it's important that the original requestor follows through or follows up so my other contact knows it's worth their time. Check out my Honor Code for Building High-Quality Career Relationships resource in the Appendix on how to connect thoughtfully. Make sure if you ask for a favor, you show up when others do for you.

There are many ways to help others and give to your professional network. Here are some of them:

Introduce people who don't know each other

When asked or when you think it makes sense, introduce two people you know through LinkedIn, email, or in person, including across internal teams at your company. Make sure you know enough about both people and their goals for connecting so you can include that detail in the message and make sure the introduction is productive for all involved. Try to give advice when the person who requested the introduction may need to research or prepare first. This will also show their willingness to make an investment and put in the work, demonstrating that this effort is important enough to them to expect time from others.

Provide resources and create opportunities

If you see articles, books, movies, or other resources that someone in your network might find helpful, pass them along. For example, I emailed a few colleagues about a conference I was attending, inviting them to join me since we had shared interest in the topic. Another time, I emailed a nonprofit consultant about a socially conscious coffee company that has a similar company name, thinking it might be in line with her work and a fun gift for her clients or her community. Recommend colleagues for speaking engagements or business opportunities that they may be a fit for.

Help with the job search

As I mentioned in Chapter 4, more than 30 percent of job applicants come through referrals. If you like helping others make connections in their job search, make sure you have enough information about the person and their experience to feel confident in recommending them for a job. If not, ask for more information, or suggest they do more research, or connect them with someone in a similar role to the one they're applying for so they can be better prepared for an interview or referral. Review someone's resume and recommend changes to make it more relevant to the job description. Describe your company's culture, what you know about the people they'll be working with, or your previous interview experience so they have insight into what to expect if or when they get to that step.

Mentor or teach

Think about mentoring as lifting others up so that we're all more impactful. Several years ago, I felt like I was just taking from others and simply doing my job, and I wanted to give more. I decided at the beginning of each year that I would create a Giving Plan, where I'd set three areas to focus on helping others for the next twelve months.[20] Annually, teaching and mentoring have been constants in my Giving Plan because I can teach a group of students at one time, multiplying my impact, and because I've become a storyteller, I can translate my professional experiences into actionable advice. If this kind of giving appeals to you, consider mentoring students, graduates, and professionals who are earlier in their careers. You can be a personal advocate in their corner, creating a safe space to share personal and professional experiences, and to gain and give advice.

Share and celebrate others' work, ideas, and stories

This is a fun one because it's easy to share someone else's great news, projects, research surveys, accomplishments, success, and even job openings. Social media makes sharing others' work to multiply the impact easy. During the height of the COVID-19 pandemic in spring 2020, I curated a list of resources, ideas, services, and advice from my community, for my community. It was a small way to help and make my social media scrolling productive to help others who were homebound, looking for ways to help themselves and others.

Redirect requests

Since I learned this from Adam Grant, I've been paying attention when others ask me for help and pointing them in a different, hopefully better, direction when I'm not the best person for the job. This is a way that you, too, can continue to help others, rather than be a dead end, and at least help them continue their journey. The most common way to redirect others is to introduce them to someone in a similar role to the one they may be pursuing, especially when you don't have relevant expertise. Of course, check with the other individual first—share details you learned from the person who contacted you to make sure the other person is open to the introduction. The answer is almost always yes. This can also be a quick, small way to make a big impact for someone else.

Volunteer and create social impact

You might contribute time, expertise, or money, such as financial donations. I give to groups and organizations meaningful to me. I've taught The Knock Method to students and nonprofit professionals through workshops, waiving registration fees, and donating the related workbooks to help them further their budding careers and missions. I support many of the groups and organizations that volunteered their stories for inclusion in this book. If you're looking to mentor, consider volunteering with Year Up.[21] If you'd like to help fight hunger, join me in contributing to Move for Hunger or other organizations you feel a pull toward.[22] If you are an artist who may be interested in depicting the story of someone who's been brushed by cancer, or you have been touched by it yourself, get involved with Twist Out Cancer or organizations that fight for those who need an extra fight or have prevailed over unimaginable health challenges.[23]

Contribute early and often

One of the tactics I used when bringing two disconnected groups together within my company was contributing something early. I brought something to the table—a document with resources our team had produced, organized by topic—to share what our team could offer to help the other team achieve their goals. This was a key turning point because I had put in effort and taken action to gather information they could react to, creating more of a conversation than an ask. Think about how you can help others through action or sharing ideas that could help them, even before you meet, to bring value from the get-go, and they'll see that you're committed to giving to the relationship.

Practice compassion in the workplace

Listen to your colleagues and contacts, and extend a hand to help them find resources, or lend an ear if you sense they may be suffering or needing support.

Practice gratitude

Being present and mindful and practicing gratitude have received growing focus related to mental health in our communities, our world, and even at work. Writing in gratitude journals has become a popular activity, by taking a few moments each day to think about positives in our lives. Consider extending your gratitude journal to include others you can thank for their help, knowledge, and support in your career and life. Research shows that practicing gratitude leads to lower levels of cellular inflammation, better sleep, and a healthier heart.[24] Find creative ways to thank those who help you along your path in ways that are meaningful to them. Practice other-centeredness, not only when reaching out to others, but when it comes to gratitude, too.[25]

\ ' /

WRAP UP:
KEEP ON KNOCKING

Build relationships that open doors,
and keep them open

Now you know the five simple steps for building high-quality, positive, and mutually beneficial career relationships, known as The Knock Method. You have learned that by intentionally approaching and nurturing each relationship with professional contacts, you are improving your health and the health of others and supporting your well-being and the well-being of others. You are even combating isolation, which contributes to a more connected and purpose-driven world. You have the confidence to quiet that inner voice of doubt that wonders if you can contribute to an interaction with someone decades your senior, compete for a role in a new industry, or connect with role models, startup founders, or nonprofit supporters. And you know that the more energy, thought, and goodwill you put into preparing for and investing in relationships, the higher quality network you can build, which elevates the impact everyone in it can make.

No more shortcuts. No more one-sided outreach requests. Using The Knock Method, you're in it for the long game of relationship building as you develop your career. Not only are you better for it, but the way you value others' lives and experiences will shine through. Networking isn't something to dread or an obligation. When you approach career relationships with care and other-centeredness and a focus on collective impact, you generate good vibes, and the more good vibes you feel, the more you'll want to keep the rhythm going. You'll achieve more success, not just in reaching your own career goals, but in helping others reach theirs, and in making a positive impact on your workplaces and communities.

> **When you approach career relationships with care and other-centeredness and a focus on collective impact, you generate good vibes, and the more good vibes you feel, the more you'll want to keep the rhythm going.**

Eric Silverstein of The Peached Tortilla sums up the lasting power of just one high-quality career connection.

During our interview, Eric and I went down memory lane from when our friendship and career relationship started in 2010. I was one of the first people he became connected to when he was new to Austin at that time, and when my Austin entertainment blog was gaining traction. Eric's friend, Charles, whom I knew because we were both bloggers, had asked if I might share some local restaurant knowledge with Eric before he brought his concept to the market. Eric reminded me in our interview that I had introduced him to another local blogger, who had then introduced Eric to the owner of the bar who gave Eric his first prime-time parking spot on Austin's famous Sixth Street for The Peached Tortilla food truck on Saturday nights, which meant lots of hungry bar-hoppers on the busiest night of the week for his budding business.

Those connections led to more connections, each helping Eric build his brand into the popular restaurant group it is today. "The web of connections from that introduction is a network of about a hundred people," he said. "Whether you realize it or not, that one connection sprouted so many other connections." He also planted other seeds that he grew his network from, and ten years later, his network of quality relationships—those he can rely on and give to—is vast. "I literally didn't know one person in Austin before that," he

> **"You took the time for me, and that was like lighting a match. That's all I needed; I needed someone to light a match for me, and I'll take it from there."**
>
> —Eric Silverstein

said. He adds that one connection can go very far if that person is a connecter themselves. It's all about that person taking time for you. "You took the time for me, and that was like lighting a match. That's all I needed; I needed someone to light a match for me, and I'll take it from there," Eric said with his innate determination and equal gratitude. But he hasn't just taken others' help and absorbed it; he's tried to repay that favor ten times over by giving his time to aspiring entrepreneurs and giving people opportunities to work for him temporarily to gain experience. He also took on the responsibility to invest himself in relationships, putting in the research and the work, following through on connections others made for him, owning his authenticity, and showcasing his genuine nature. And he keeps giving, no matter how much success he achieves or how busy his day is. Eric took the time to conduct our interview while he was fighting to keep his business afloat and sailing during the COVID-19 pandemic, which hit restaurants especially hard. But he makes time to keep lighting the match and making the powerful flame of connection even brighter and illuminating the path for others.

This is the kind of cycle that The Knock Method can generate.

As you need help, high-quality connections can launch you to the next opportunity. As you gain knowledge and establish yourself, you'll keep giving to your relationships and connections, fortifying your collective web of talent, experience, and personal interactions. Along the way, don't forget to recognize yourself and others who are working toward better outcomes for everyone, giving as you learn, sharing your knowledge as you invest yourself in career experiences, and creating impact for others while you craft your own meaningful career.

Let's recap some of the main themes covered in *Knock*.

1. **Practice other-centeredness and shift focus off of yourself and onto others.** The Knock Method centers around the notion that career relationships are "not about me." Always think one step ahead of an interaction or communication with a professional contact. Listen. Think about how you can make the interaction more about them and what you can do together, rather than focusing exclusively on your individual goals.

2. **Quality relationships are healthy for us.** Acting as an imposter to yourself—doing things counter to your values and gut feeling—causes distress, while positive relationships contribute to greater well-being, including healthier blood pressure and heart rates.

3. **The Knock Method shortens the gap between you and your professional contacts, regardless of role or level of experience.** Investing yourself in relationships also shortens the gap and creates a bridge between where you are now and where you want to be.

4. **Prepare to connect.** Research, which helps you to know your topic and your contact before you meet, prepares you for a more thoughtful interaction with your contacts. It helps you zero in on the right opportunities and filter out the ones that aren't a fit, ensuring a more valuable time spent for all involved.

5. **Use specifics and answer questions before they are asked.** Put in the work to answer this question for your contact: "Why would you want to interact with me?"

6. **Help them help you.** Make it easy for someone to connect with you. Explain why you're reaching out as it relates to what's important to *them* (your research will help you uncover this), put meeting times in their time zone, or meet them at their event or their office, for example.

7. **Think about *when* to implement The Knock Method steps**— before, during, or after an interaction with a professional contact.

8. **Create an experience, not an exchange.** Instead of a this-for-that perspective, think about what you can create and do together, and how much more powerful your experiences, perspectives, and skills are combined.

9. **Follow up and follow through.** You put the work in *before* an interaction, so don't forget—it's equally important to put in effort *after* the interaction to keep the relationship going and growing. Practice gratitude, thank those who help you and others, and keep giving to others in your path.

10. **Redirect as a way to help and give, and prioritize compassion in the workplace.** Listen and ask questions to identify the best way to help an individual. Sometimes, that means

redirecting them to someone or a resource that is better positioned to help them succeed. The effectiveness of a mentoring relationship relies on the dedication and consistency of the mentor's giving. Practice compassion in the workplace by responding to others' suffering on a human level. Because we spend so much time in the workplace, compassion has a lasting impact on the lives of others by making business more human and is critical to a healthy work environment that is not only good for business, but also the world we shape and share.

WHAT'S NEXT?

For each step of The Knock Method, you have discovered ways to learn more about potential connections and ways to shift focus off of yourself and onto others. Now, here are some exercises and resources to help you get started right away in putting The Knock Method into action beyond the pages of this book, in face-to-face interactions and real-world business scenarios.

STEP 1: KNOW MY TOPIC AND MY CONTACT
Take Action

- Get to know your contacts *before* you connect. This helps enrich your time together, uncover commonality, and find ways to relate.

- Use publicly available tools like search engines to look for their name in the news, follow them on social media, or look them up on internal company organization charts.

- Ask mutual contacts about your contacts to familiarize yourself with who they are and their work experience to home in on valuable ways to help each other.

EXERCISES/RESOURCES
Use these resources, all available in the Appendix, to prepare before connecting with career contacts.

- 10 Ways to Find People to Connect With (Resource #2)

- 10 Research Tactics (Resource #3)

- When to Reach Out to Connect (Resource #4)

- 15 Questions to Answer before Reaching Out (Resource #5)

- Outreach Message Framework (Resource #6)

STEP 2: NOT ABOUT ME
Take Action

- Find ways to help others through everyday activities.

- Share someone's article with your network online, reach out to someone you've worked with to see how they're doing, or ask people at work what organizations they're a part of and what's important to them out of the office.

- Get involved in organizations that make an important impact with a cause that's meaningful to you.

- Support businesses who have a mission you support when you buy products or pay for services. For example, if you are moving, you could find a mover at Move for Hunger, which donates nonperishable food items that would otherwise go to waste to local food banks. Do the research to find companies that have a social impact arm so you know you're supporting important causes—like environmental protection, safe worker conditions, or community relief funds—during checkout for online purchases. Conduct business in a way that makes an impact because of the globally conscious companies and individuals you partner and work with.

EXERCISES/RESOURCES
Use these resources, all available in the Appendix, to help you focus on your contacts and the impact you can have together.

- 10 Ways to Find People to Connect With (Resource #2)

- 10 Research Tactics (Resource #3)

- 15 Questions to Answer before Reaching Out (Resource #5)

- Mentoring Honor Code (Resource #10)

STEP 3: OWN IT
Take Action

- Practice authenticity by sharing more about yourself at the beginning of work meetings, dedicating time on calls for introductions, and taking note of personal details others share too, so you can share and get to know the humans behind your work.

- Get involved in organizations where you can practice authenticity and embrace vulnerability. For example, if you or a loved one has been touched by cancer, you could support an organization like Twist Out Cancer.

- For career opportunities you're pursuing, invest (put the work in) by getting to know people who have experience in that role, on that team, or at that company. Offer to volunteer for a project above and beyond your daily responsibilities to get your feet wet and learn the landscape.

- Sign up for free trials of technology that you'd like to learn how to use or that job descriptions expect and require. Volunteer at industry conferences to immerse yourself in a field and to gain knowledge and experience that can prove you've invested in an opportunity and that can equip you for interviews. *Do* what you want to be doing. Practice. Get your feet wet.

- Before you connect with others, invest in the relationship up front by engaging with articles they've written by leaving a comment or sharing it on your social networks, buying someone's book, listening to their podcast, attending their event, or buying their product so you can connect with them on a deeper level.

EXERCISES/RESOURCES

Use this resource, available in the Appendix, to help you *own it*—to bring your most authentic self and invest in relationships by preparing how you show up in them.

- The Concentric Circles exercise can help you prepare how you reveal layers of your true self before joining a meeting or meeting someone new. (Resource #8)

STEP 4: COMMONALITY
Take Action

Read how Eric Silverstein, founder of The Peached Tortilla restaurant concepts, used commonality to focus less on competition and more on friendship with his primary competitor.[1]

EXERCISES/RESOURCES

Use this resource in the Appendix to explore how to open the door with commonality.

- The Concentric Circles exercise (Resource #8) can help you define your personal brand. It prepares you to connect with others and helps you practice authenticity to reveal more about yourself that others can remember and relate to. It helps you differentiate yourself and come prepared with topics you can bring up when first connecting with others so they can get to know the real you.

STEP 5: KEEP GIVING
Take Action

- Explore how you can help make your company or organization more positive with high-quality interactions. You can learn more about how to develop interactions like these through the Center for Positive Organizations at the University of Michigan. Consider joining its Positive Organizations Consortium or executive education programs like Practicing Positive Leadership.

- Consider mentoring young professionals through programs like Year Up to share your experience and provide a quality, consistent relationship for someone who can benefit as they develop their career.

- Share on your interoffice profile or social media profiles that you are a mentor so others know they can reach out for career advice, whether for a specific career situation or to get to know each other and possibly nurture the relationship into a long-term mentoring one.

- Set up an account with TimeTrade[2] or Calendly,[3] which gives you a link to add to your social profiles and emails for others to find an open time on your calendar. It's an easy way to make yourself available and share your open time slots to avoid going back and forth trying to nail down a meeting time.

EXERCISES/RESOURCES
Use these resources, all available in the Appendix, to practice generosity and gratitude with others.

- Mentoring Honor Code (Resource #10)

- 10 Ways to Follow Up after Connecting (Resource #11)—Use as a refresher after interactions with professional contacts to keep the relationship going.

- "Gratitude Journal: A Collection of 67 Templates, Ideas, and Apps for Your Diary"[4]—Learn about the power of gratitude and how to practice it in this article on positivepsychology.com.

- Visit theknockmethod.com[5] to download a badge you can add to your professional social media profiles, website, or email signature to signal you are open for high-quality career conversations and you're at the door, ready to answer for those who knock (after they thoughtfully prepare, of course).

BEFORE, DURING, AND AFTER RESOURCES

Here's another view of the resources in the Appendix to guide you before, during, and after interactions with professional contacts.

BEFORE

- The Knock Method Honor Code for Building High-Quality Career Relationships (Resource #1)

- 10 Ways to Find People to Connect With (Resource #2)

- 10 Research Tactics (Resource #3)

- When to Reach Out to Connect (Resource #4)

- 15 Questions to Answer before Reaching Out (Resource #5)

- Outreach Message Framework (Resource #6)

- 50 Informal Interview Questions (Resource #7)

- Concentric Circles Exercise (Resource #8)

- You Are What You Prepare (Resource #9)

- Mentoring Honor Code (Resource #10)

DURING

- The Knock Method Honor Code for Building High-Quality Career Relationships (Resource #1)

- 50 Informational Interview Questions (Resource #7)

- Mentoring Honor Code (Resource #10)

AFTER

- The Knock Method Honor Code for Building High-Quality Career Relationships (Resource #1)

- Mentoring Honor Code (Resource #10)

- 10 Ways to Follow Up after Connecting (Resource #11)

READY, SET, (PREPARE), KNOCK

The power that lies in the steps and stories that make up The Knock Method doesn't come to life curled up in a reading chair at home. You'll need to apply it in everyday interactions online, at work, and in collaborative meetings. If you're reading this on an airplane, while waiting for your next virtual meeting, in line (maybe even six feet apart) for coffee, or on the beach, a new high-quality connection may be just within reach. People like you and those you connect with, and how you interact together for the greater good, are what drive The Knock Method's success. It takes time to incorporate it into your communications and relationships, and to practice it until it feels natural and your confidence begins to solidify. The more you incorporate it into your work and life, the more positive and impactful energy and progress you'll manifest around you, and now you won't be surprised when it makes you feel great!

You might think of The Knock Method as a mentality, a shift in mindset that becomes part of your lifestyle, or a way of conducting business with a more human-centric focus. While much of it may take place in remote interactions through video conferencing, phone calls, and even social media, resist the urge to use screens as shields. Digital screens, just like open doors that will come from you thoughtfully knocking, are a gateway to meaningful relationships if you focus on quality interactions, listening, and finding ways to create opportunities and value for others.

That's why I've created a community—think of it as a neighborhood with an open-door policy—for *Knock* readers and The Knock Method workshop participants that you can tap into to soak up more goodness, stories, and inspiration from The Knock Method. I invite you to visit theknockmethod.com[6] to find and connect with others who are adopting this mindset and relationship-building work style. You can also download The Knock Method digital badge to signal to others that your "door" is open for knocking and that you're ready to be a resource for others as they develop their careers, which will undoubtedly create and nurture connections and open many more doors for you too.

Once you close the back flap of this book, come join The Knock Method community and take this other-centered approach from concept to reality. Here's how:

1. **Soak up more stories, science, and strategies.** Visit theknock-method.com, where you can read, watch, and listen to stories about successful professionals who have built their success through building high-quality relationships. This digital destination also offers insight into the psychology research that backs The Knock Method, so you can delve into the science behind the power of connection and how it can help you develop impactful relationships as you develop your career. You better bet The Knock Method community will want to hear and learn from your success stories about how you put the steps into practice and the outcomes you achieved. Come share with us!

2. **Join and request virtual and in-person workshops.** Sign up for an in-person or virtual workshop to meet other students and professionals who value high-quality relationships for meaningful career development and who practice The Knock Method in actual work scenarios. You can request a workshop for a particular group or event too, for students and professionals looking to bring more intentional career relationships to make their work more meaningful and fulfilling.

3. **The Knock Method digital badge program.** Signal to others on your LinkedIn profile, website, email signature, or digital portfolio that you are a resource for others, you

are open to career conversations, and you're committed to building others up as you develop your own career. Hey, it'll be a conversation starter, too, for career conversations and even interviews.

4. **Buy a book, gift a book!** Excited about the ideas and how-tos you just absorbed by learning The Knock Method? When you buy a gift for yourself or someone else, go the extra mile to bring Step 5: *Keep Giving* to life and buy two! Pay it forward. Lift someone up. Share your newfound confidence. Think of a student, friend, colleague, family member, or high-quality career connection that you owe a thank-you and send one their way. For a digital version, Amazon makes it easy to send an e-book gift to someone else by email for them to redeem on their device.

All right, *career builders*, *career growers*, and *career changers*. You have everything you need to intentionally build high-quality, positive, mutually beneficial career relationships—to open doors and keep them open as you develop your career.

Just think, at this very moment, there are people in your orbit that you may have crossed paths with and those you have yet to—closed doors with future career contacts that you have the power to open when you thoughtfully knock. When you open doors to deep career relationships with undefined, yet boundless collective potential, what will you achieve? And when others knock, how will you answer?

APPENDIX

READY-TO-USE RESOURCES

	STEP 1 Know my topic, my contact, and specifics up front. Prepare to connect.	STEP 2 Not about me. Focus on my contacts, us, and our mutual impact.	STEP 3 Own it. Be personal and authentic; invest in the relationship and the cause up front.	STEP 4 Commonality. Build trust to open the door.	STEP 5 Keep giving. Help others and practice generosity and gratitude.
#1: The Knock Method Honor Code for Building High-Quality Career Relationships	BEFORE	BEFORE DURING AFTER	BEFORE DURING AFTER	BEFORE DURING AFTER	BEFORE DURING AFTER
#2: 10 Ways to Find People to Connect With	BEFORE	BEFORE			
#3: 10 Research Tactics	BEFORE	BEFORE			
#4: When to Reach Out to Connect	BEFORE				
#5: 15 Questions to Answer Before Reaching Out	BEFORE	BEFORE			
#6: Outreach Message Framework	BEFORE				
#7: 50 Informational Interview Questions	BEFORE	DURING			DURING
#8: Concentric Circles Exercise			BEFORE	BEFORE	
#9: You Are What You Prepare		BEFORE			
#10: Mentoring Honor Code	BEFORE	BEFORE DURING AFTER	BEFORE DURING AFTER	BEFORE DURING	DURING
#11: 10 Ways to Follow Up After Connecting					AFTER

RESOURCE #1:
THE KNOCK METHOD HONOR CODE FOR BUILDING HIGH-QUALITY CAREER RELATIONSHIPS

1. I will only reach out when I have intent to follow up and follow through.

2. I will take the initiative to set up the time, location to meet.

3. I will be on time and respect the time another is giving to me.

4. I will send information prior to an interaction if it will save the other time and help us have a more productive conversation.

5. I will uncover common ground and prepare to connect to provide immediate value up front and build trust.

6. I will have topics of conversation prepared prior to meeting, but be open to allow the conversation to expand to uncover partnership possibilities.

7. I will share ideas for the other person, partners, or group members to help them in their endeavors.

8. I will thank everyone who lends time, energy, earned experience and follow up on actions discussed.

9. I will respond to introductions from mutual contacts within 48 hours (goal) to honor the person(s) who introduced us and punctuate merit in my asks, or pursuits that warranted the introduction.

10. I will acknowledge when an interaction or connection isn't adding value or making the most of another's time, and suggest a resource or person who may be a better fit, or save them time by cutting it short and thanking them for their time.

11. I will ask questions about an ask from someone else to determine if I'm the best fit to help them, and if not, provide ideas to redirect them in the right direction.

12. I will accept that sometimes I catch someone at an inopportune time and may not even hear back. Following up never hurts.

13. I will respect that everyone has different priorities and they may not be aligned with mine at a given time.

14. I will share clarifying information when someone I reach out to may not understand the value I think we may be able to provide to each other.

15. I will follow up respectfully, after some time, if I don't hear from someone to provide another opportunity to collaborate, in case I caught them at a bad time.

16. I will practice gratitude and compassion for myself when I take risks to reach out to connect, regardless of the outcome.

17. I will forgive myself for times when I don't get an interaction quite right and will make efforts to correct it.

18. I will provide specifics up front when connecting with others, including specific times/days/locations to meet to save them time, another email, and make it easy to connect.

19. I will think about how I can help those I connect with, and who they may find benefit from connecting with in my network.

20. I will think more about long-term possibilities of connecting than about instrumental, give-to-get interactions. (Ex: For every interview that doesn't result in a job, that's one company or recruiter to stay in touch with for future interactions)

RESOURCE #2:
10 WAYS TO FIND PEOPLE TO CONNECT WITH

1. Read industry best-of lists (e.g., "Top Companies to Work For").

2. Attend industry events, conferences, meetings.

3. Subscribe to newsletters; reach out to those featured or contributing authors.

4. Ask your network of friends and colleagues.

5. Follow hashtags on social channels.

6. Sign up for Google Alerts with keywords.

7. Search online for businesses near you with a similar concept.

8. Use LinkedIn search with keyword combos.

9. Reach out to industry associations and ask to visit an event before joining.

10. Read the news about your topic of interest.

GOAL: Discover people and companies that align with your interests to connect with and uncover ways to help each other.

RESOURCE #3:
10 RESEARCH TACTICS

1. LinkedIn—Contact Tab>Website/Portfolio

2. Search Twitter for a person or company.

3. Search Facebook for a person or company.

4. Search Instagram for a person or company.

5. Conduct a news search about your contact on Google.

6. Use keywords on Google Alerts.

7. Ask a mutual friend.

8. Read a person's or a company's publications.

9. Watch videos of their work.

10. Attend an event they are speaking at.

GOAL: Know your contact's work. Gather context.

RESOURCE #4:
WHEN TO REACH OUT TO CONNECT

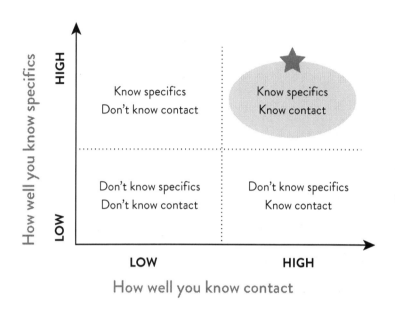

GOAL: Develop confidence that you're prepared and it's the right time to reach out.

RESOURCE #5:
15 QUESTIONS TO ANSWER BEFORE REACHING OUT (ANSWER ANY OR ALL)

1. Who is the contact?

2. Where do they live?

3. Where are they right now (e.g., they might be traveling for work)?

4. What is their personal brand like?

5. What are their likes/dislikes?

6. What are their social channels?

7. Do they have a website/portfolio? What is it?

8. Have they won awards or had work recognized? If so, which ones?

9. How do you know them? Take note of specific sources (e.g., I read about you in X publication).

10. How did you find them?

11. What do you know about them?

12. Who can connect you?

13. How can you do something together? And why do you think so?

14. What are the answers to common possible questions that they will want to ask you?

15. How is this potential partnership cool, fun, helpful, impactful?

GOAL: Prepare to connect by unlocking what's important to your contact, even before you connect.

RESOURCE #6:
OUTREACH MESSAGE FRAMEWORK

Compelling subject line or message	*(Impact, Other-Centeredness, Commonality)*
Friendly greeting and personal comment	*(Other-Centeredness, Commonality)*
MAIN BODY State why you are reaching out, how you know about them, and your particular interest in them.	*(Authenticity, Commonality, Investment)*
Highlight how you can work together for a great outcome.	*(Impact)*
Include details from your research to preemptively answer their questions.	*(Research, Specifics, Investment)*
CONCLUSION Ask to connect with specific options and methods.	*(Research, Specifics, Other-Centeredness, Gratitude)*

GOAL: To open the door to connect versus to get a quick response to an ask.

RESOURCE #7:
50 INFORMATIONAL INTERVIEW QUESTIONS

Current Role/Career

1. Can you describe your current role and how you found it?

2. How does a typical day in this role go?

3. What do you like most about your company?

4. What's the company culture like where you work?

5. What are some of the unique company benefits you take advantage of?

6. What's a current challenge you're facing at work, and what steps are you taking to overcome it?

7. What's the most recent project you worked on, and what impact is it making?

8. Describe a time when you asked for something at work and didn't receive it.

9. Describe a time when you asked for something at work and did receive it.

10. Can you tell me about a time when you worked on a project and it didn't turn out as expected? What was the outcome or lesson learned?

11. Can you think of a time when you were surprised in your career?

12. What's your advice for someone looking to switch roles, industries, careers?

13. What is (are) your current career goals(s)?

14. What's the review and growth process like on your team/at your company?

15. How do you define success in your role?

16. What strategies do you use to drive your career growth?

17. What are some big initiatives at your company right now (that you can speak about)?

Education

1. How does/doesn't your education play into your current career?

2. What publications or media are you most interested in currently?

3. How do you stay up to date with industry news?

4. What education opportunities, workshops, or courses would you recommend to learn more about this industry or skill?

Mentorship

1. How did you go about finding mentors to guide you along your career?

2. Who is one mentor who's made an impact on you and how?

3. What advice have you been given that guides your career?

> **PRO TIP:** Pick one to three questions that you definitely want to ask in a thirty-minute conversation, and then have several backup questions.

Personal

1. How do you work toward achieving work/life balance?

2. What are your strategies for taking breaks throughout the workday?

3. How do you organize your workday?

4. What activities are you involved in outside of work?

5. How do you keep up with multiple interests and position them to create your personal brand?

6. Do you tend to focus on one area of expertise or a varied set of skills and interests?

7. What do you look forward to most in your personal or professional life?

8. What accomplishment are you most proud of?

9. Describe a time in your career or life when something didn't work out like you wanted it to and what the outcome was.

Interviewing

1. What's the toughest interview question you've ever been asked?

2. Do you have any suggestions on how to respectfully negotiate a salary?

3. What are your top 1–3 interviewing tips?

4. What are your top 1–3 things to avoid in an interview?

5. What's your best/most interesting interview story?

6. What are your top 1–3 resume writing tips for success?

7. What are your top 1–3 things to avoid in resume writing?

8. What do you look for in a resume to determine if you should bring in a candidate to interview?

9. Could you share mistakes from an interview that you learned from?

10. What are your tips for staying focused and patient during the waiting game after interviews?

11. What's the best way to prepare for an upcoming interview at your company?

Expanding Your Network

1. Who are some of the most connected people in your professional network that you look up to and why?

2. How do you stay connected with key contacts in your network?

3. Which industry or professional organizations or events do you recommend to get more connected in my career?

4. Based on my background and interests, is there anyone that you recommend I meet and why? (Don't forget to ask for an introduction.)

5. Do you have tips for expanding your network in a new city or region?

6. What's the best way for us to stay connected?

RESOURCE #8:
CONCENTRIC CIRCLES EXERCISE

1. Think about how you can share your authentic self with others to provide more points on which you can both connect. Aim for the center of the circles (see the figure that follows) by reaching out to connect. Then, make an ask.

2. By opening the door for dialogue (the inner two circles), you can create more possibilities for you and your contact to help each other and develop a more lasting relationship than if you had only stayed in the outer circle or simply made your ask.

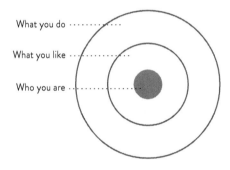

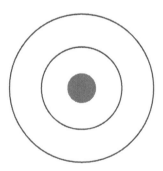

RESOURCE #9:
YOU ARE WHAT YOU PREPARE

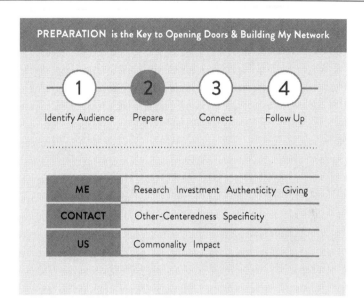

GOAL: Double down on preparing to connect. Putting in more work up front sets you and your contact up for a productive interaction. Spend 70 percent preparing, 20 percent connecting, and 10 percent following up.

RESOURCE #10:
MENTORING HONOR CODE

The mentor

1. I will go into a mentoring relationship with a focus on my own accountability, knowing that success depends heavily on me with the sole goal to support others as they develop their careers.

2. I will attend the meetings those I mentor set with me, based on times we agree on together.

3. I will communicate with those I mentor if major conflicts arise, and I will make every effort to reschedule to prioritize consistent support for them.

4. I will work with those I mentor to set expectations for our relationship at the start and reevaluate as it evolves.

5. I will follow through and provide resources, advice, and introductions that I offer to those I mentor.

6. I will look for opportunities to support those I mentor and resources or connections that can help them progress.

7. I will provide positive feedback and constructive feedback to those I mentor, and celebrate their successes with them.

8. I will act as a neutral guide for those I mentor, providing the support they ask for in a way that's most helpful for them, and be their advocate.

9. I will check in on and look out for the well-being of those I mentor, and will seek resources to help them when their needs exceed my ability to provide what they need.

10. I will share with others the benefits of positive, high-quality mentoring relationships so that others are inspired to

serve as a mentor or to seek out and nurture high-quality mentoring relationships so that all of our careers are strengthened by having someone to turn to and in our corner as we develop our careers.

The one being mentored

1. I will be specific in what I ask my mentor to support me with.

2. I will ask my mentor for help and not assume they know how they can support me.

3. I will proactively prepare and present my goals and desired outcomes from our professional relationship with my mentor.

4. I will set up times to meet that work for both of us on a consistent basis.

5. I will come to meetings with topics to discuss with my mentor.

6. I will take my mentor's advice and guidance and try to apply it, and then share what I learned.

7. I will communicate with my mentor when obligations take over and I'm not able to give to the relationship some days, weeks, or months (and give myself permission to accept changing priorities).

8. I will thank my mentor, but also know that trying my best in career situations and applying feedback is likely the only expectation and wish that they have.

9. I will accept my mentor's guidance with gratitude and know that by learning from them, I can pay it forward to others in the future.

RESOURCE #11:
10 WAYS TO FOLLOW UP AFTER CONNECTING

1. Send an email or handwritten thank-you note with a recap of your meeting.

2. Call your contact to thank them.

3. Introduce them to contacts mentioned in your conversation or that come to mind.

4. Send a relevant resource, article, or video to them.

5. Invite them to an upcoming event and cover a ticket.

6. Send a gift (if appropriate)—maybe even a copy of *Knock* (*hint, hint*).

7. Feature them in an article, project, or event.

8. Offer up some social media love.

9. Set up a recurring touch-base reminder.

10. Send them a birthday greeting.

GOAL: Keep the door open, and keep giving to further develop and nurture your high-quality mutually beneficial relationships.

NOTES

A NEW WAY TO KNOCK

1. Wolcott College Prep (website), accessed October 14, 2020, https:// wolcottschool.org

2. "Green Ribbon Schools," U.S. Department of Education, September 18, 2018, https://wolcottschool.org/wp-content/uploads/2018/09/EDGRS -State-Release-Wolcott.pdf

3. "Program Rankings," The University of Texas at Austin McCombs School of Business, accessed October 14, 2020, https://www.mccombs .utexas.edu/About/Rankings

4. Katie Hafner, "How Thursday Became the New Friday," *New York Times* online, November 6, 2005, https://www.nytimes.com/2005/11/06 /us/education/how-thursday-became-the-new-friday.html

5. "'Shallow' Best Song *A Star Is Born* 2019 Oscars," Interview with Lady Gaga, *Variety*, February 24, 2019, https://www.youtube.com /watch?v=9dFhyO1GDRw

6. Link building is the process of acquiring hyperlinks from other websites to your own; Paddy Moogan, "The Beginner's Guide to Link Building," MOZ, accessed October 14, 2020, https://moz.com/beginners-guide-to -link-building

HOW DO YOU FEEL WHEN YOU KNOCK?

1.   "Center for Positive Organizations," University of Michigan Ross School of Business, accessed October 14, 2020, https://positiveorgs.bus .umich.edu/

2.   Definition of loneliness: Stephen Trzeciak and Anthony Mazzarelli, *Compassionomics: The Revolutionary Scientific Evidence That Caring Makes a Difference* (Pensacola, FL: Studer Group, 2019), 49; "A Whole Host of Health Risks": Julianne Holt-Lunstad and Timothy B. Smith, "Loneliness and Social Isolation as Risk Factors for CVD: Implications for Evidence-Based Patient Care and Scientific Inquiry," *Heart* 102, no. 13 (July 1, 2016): 987–9, https://heart.bmj.com/content/102/13/987; Stephanie Cacioppo, Angela J. Grippo, Sarah London, and John T. Cacioppo, "Loneliness: Clinical Import and Interventions," *Perspectives on Psychological Science* 10, no. 2 (2015): 238–49, https:// doi.org/10.1177/1745691615570616; Vivek H. Murthy, *Together: The Healing Power of Human Connection in a Sometimes Lonely World* (New York: Harper Collins, 2020), 8.

3.   Julianne Holt-Lunstad, Timothy B. Smith, Mark Baker, et al., "Loneliness and Social Isolation as Risk Factors for Mortality: A Meta-Analytic Review," *Perspectives on Psychological Science* 10, no. 2 (2015): 227–37, doi: 10.1177/1745691614568352; Julianne Holt-Lunstad, Timothy B. Smith, J. Bradley Layton, "Social Relationships and Mortality Risk: A Meta-Analytic Review," *PLOS Medicine* 7, no. 7 (July 27, 2010), doi: e1000316; Trzeciak and Mazzarelli, *Compassionomics*, 49.

4.   Trzeciak and Mazzarelli, *Compassionomics*, 49; Murthy, *Together*.

5.   Holt-Lunstad, Smith, Baker, et al., "Loneliness and Social Isolation as Risk Factors for Mortality," 227–37; Trzeciak and Mazzarelli, *Compassionomics*, 49.

6.   Holt-Lunstad, Smith, Layton, "Social Relationships and Mortality Risk."

7.   Brené Brown, "America's Crisis of Disconnection Runs Deeper Than Politics," *Fast Company*, September 12, 2017, https://www .fastcompany.com/40465644/brene-brown-americas-crisis-of -disconnection-runs-deeper-than-politics

8. Trzeciak and Mazzarelli, *Compassionomics*, 49.

9. Murthy, *Together*, xxii.

10. Dr. Jane Dutton and Dr. Emily Heaphy say positive social interactions are "characterized by the pursuit of rewarding and desired outcomes, whereas negative ones are characterized by unwelcome and punishing outcomes." Emily D. Heaphy and Jane E. Dutton, "Positive Social Interactions and the Human Body at Work: Linking Organizations and Physiology," *Academy of Management Review* 33, no. 1 (2008): 139, https://doi.org/10.5465/amr.2008.27749365

11. Murthy, *Together*. Quality connections improve your health and reduce health risks and severity/recovery. On the surface, supportive people will help you when you need compassion. Deeper down, being surrounded by positive and high-quality relationships at work improve your physiological health.

12. Heaphy and Dutton, "Positive Social Interactions and the Human Body at Work," 143.

13. Monica C. Worline and Jane E. Dutton, *Awakening Compassion at Work: The Quiet Power That Elevates People and Organizations* (Oakland, CA: Berrett-Koehler Publishers, 2017).

14. Trzeciak and Mazzarelli, *Compassionomics*, 54; Citation 92, Steve W. Cole, Louise C. Hawkley, Jesusa M. Arevalo, Caroline Y. Sung, Robert M. Rose, and John T. Cacioppo, "Social Regulation of Gene Expression in Human Leukocytes," *Genome Biology* 8, no. 9 (2007): R189.

15. Tom Rath and Jim Harter, *Wellbeing: The Five Essential Elements* (New York: Gallup Press, 2010), 39.

16. Rath and Harter, *Wellbeing*, 34.

17. Rath and Harter, *Wellbeing*, 35.

18. Heaphy and Dutton, "Positive Social Interactions and the Human Body at Work," 140.

19. Ibid.

20. Arie Nadler in his article, "Personality and Help Seeking: Autonomous versus Dependent Seeking of Help," says: "Seeking assistance may be associated [in people's minds] with an open admission of failure and

dependence on others. These anticipated psychological costs often hinder the seeking of help, which may result in the intensification of the problem." Arie Nadler, "Personality and Help Seeking," in: G.R. Pierce, B. Lakey, I.G. Sarason, B.R. Sarason (eds.) *Sourcebook of Social Support and Personality. The Springer Series in Social/Clinical Psychology* (Boston: Springer, 1997), https://doi.org/10.1007/978-1 -4899-1843-7_17

21.   "People's readiness to seek and receive help as affected by two basic psychological needs: the need for belongingness (Baumeister & Leary, 1995), and the need for independence (Ryan & Deci, 2000). The feeling of belongingness with others constitutes the psychological glue that makes social life possible. It is the basis of social solidarity that binds people in dyadic relationships and in groups (Reicher & Haslam, 2009). It is felt by almost all of us toward our close family members and by many of us toward larger groups, such as groups of co-workers and friends." From Arie Nadler, "Personality and Help Seeking," in: Pierce, Lakey, Sarason, and Sarason (eds.) *Sourcebook of Social Support and Personality* and Arie Nadler, "The Other Side of Helping: Seeking and Receiving Help," *The Oxford Handbook of Prosocial Behavior*, David A. Schroeder and William G. Graziano, eds. (London: Oxford University Press, 2015), 1, https://www.researchgate .net/publication/318876735_The_Other_Side_of_Helping_Seeking _and_Receiving_Help_of_a_single_chapter_of_a_title_in_Oxford _Handbooks_Online_for_personal_use_for_details_see_Privacy_Policy

22.   Lifeway, accessed October 14, 2020, https://lifewaykefir.com.

CHAPTER 1

1.   Holly Firestone, "Let's Celebrate 1,000 Trailblazer Community Groups and Say #ThanksTrailblazers Together," Salesforce, June 25, 2019, https://www.salesforce.com/blog/2019/06/1000-trailblazer-community -groups.html

2.   Autumn Molay and Ryan Williams, "In-Home Data Usage Increases During Coronavirus Pandemic," Comscore, March 24, 2020, https:// www.comscore.com/Insights/Blog/In-Home-Data-Usage-Increases -During-Coronavirus-Pandemic

CHAPTER 2

1. Move for Hunger, accessed October 14, 2020, https://moveforhunger.org/

2. "Individualism," AlleyDog.com, accessed October 14, 2020, https://www.alleydog.com/glossary/definition.php?term=Individualism

3. "Individualism versus Collectivism," Future Learn, accessed October 14, 2020, https://www.futurelearn.com/courses/develop-cultural-intelligence/0/steps/49772

4. Jean Twenge, "Millennials: The Me, Me, Me Generation," *Time*, May 20, 2013, https://time.com/247/millennials-the-me-me-me-generation

5. Kira M. Newman, "The Surprisingly Boring Truth about Millennials and Narcissism," *Greater Good Magazine*, January 17, 2018, https://greatergood.berkeley.edu/article/item/the_surprisingly_boring_truth_about_millennials_and_narcissism

6. "Increasing Individualism in US Linked with Rise in White-Collar Jobs," *Association for Psychological Science*, February 5, 2015, https://www.psychologicalscience.org/news/releases/increasing-individualism-in-us-linked-with-rise-of-white-collar-jobs.html

7. Heather Long, "The New Normal: 4 Job Changes by the Time You're 32," CNN Business, April 12, 2016, https://money.cnn.com/2016/04/12/news/economy/millennials-change-jobs-frequently/index.html

8. Abigail Marsh, "Could a More Individualistic World Also Be a More Altruistic One?" NPR, February 5, 2018, https://www.npr.org/sections/13.7/2018/02/05/581873428/could-a-more-individualistic-world-also-be-a-more-altruistic-one

9. "#OptOutside," REI Co-op, accessed October 14, 2020, https://www.rei.com/opt-outside

10. National Day of Unplugging, accessed October 14, 2020, https://www.nationaldayofunplugging.com

11. Keith Jensen, "Prosociality," *Current Biology* 26, no. 16 (August 22, 2016), https://pubmed.ncbi.nlm.nih.gov/27554648

12. Kristen A. Dunfield, "A Construct Divided: Prosocial Behavior as Helping, Sharing, and Comforting Subtypes," *Frontiers in Psychology* 5 (September 2014), https://www.reasearchgate.net /publication/265735594_A_construct_divided_Prosocial_behavior_as _helping_sharing_and_comforting_subtypes

13. Michael Tomasello, *Why We Cooperate* (Cambridge, MA: Massachusetts Institute of Technology, 2009), https://books.google.com /books?id=UKPxkqLGtBgC&lpg=PT7&ots=LejZCybH0E&lr&pg= PT3#v=onepage&q&f=false

14. Domen Bajde, "Other-Centered Behavior and the Dialectics of Self and Other," *Consumption, Markets, and Culture* 9, no. 4 (December 2006): 307, https://www.academia.edu/1852605/Other_centered_behavior _and_the_dialectics_of_self_and_other; referencing Alain Caille, "The double inconceivability of the pure gift," *Angelaki: Journal of the Theoretical Humanities* 6, no. 2 (2001): 23–39.

15. "Social Impact Theory Definition," accessed October 14, 2020, http:// psychology.iresearchnet.com/social-psychology/social-psychology -theories/social-impact-theory

16. Srikumar S. Rao, "Moving From a 'Me' to an 'Other-Centered' Universe," *Huffington Post*, November 17, 2011, https://www.huffpost .com/entry/how-to-be-happy-moving-fr_b_570730

17. "Adam Grant," TED, accessed October 14, 2020, https://www.ted .com/speakers/adam_grant

CHAPTER 3

1. Twist Out Cancer, accessed October 14, 2020, https://twistoutcancer.org/

2. Francesca Gino, Maryam Kouchaki, and Adam D. Galinsky, "The Moral Virtue of Authenticity: How Inauthenticity Produces Feelings of Immorality and Impurity," *Psychological Science* 26, no. 7 (2015): 983–996, https://www.hbs.edu/faculty/Publication%20Files/Moral%20 Virtue_7caef67d-e4c7-4b38-88c7-b98da81826a5.pdf, referencing Susan Harter, "Authenticity," in C.R. Snyder and S.J. Lopez, eds., *Handbook of Positive Psychology* (London: Oxford University Press, 2002), 382–394;

Alex M. Wood, P. Alex Linley, John Maltby, Michael Baliousis, and Stephen Joseph, "The Authentic Personality: A Theoretical and Empirical Conceptualization and the Development of the Authenticity Scale," *Journal of Counseling Psychology* 55, no. 3 (2008): 385–399, http://newcode.ru/lib/exe/fetch.php/authenticity_scale.pdf

3. "To Thine Own Self: The Psychology of Authenticity," *Association for Psychological Science* (blog), January 23, 2015, https://www.psychologicalscience.org/news/were-only-human/to-thine-own-self-the-psychology-of-authenticity.html

4. Adam Galinsky, "How to Speak Up for Yourself," TEDxNewYork, September 2016, https://www.ted.com/talks/adam_galinsky_how_to_speak_up_for_yourself?language=en

5. Andy Crestodina, *Content Chemistry: The Illustrated Handbook for Content Marketing* (Orbit Media Studios, 2012), https://www.amazon.com/Content-Chemistry-Illustrated-Handbook-Marketing/dp/0988336464

CHAPTER 4

1. The Peached Tortilla, accessed October 14, 2020, http://www.thepeachedtortilla.com/

2. "Signed Cookbook," The Peached Tortilla, accessed October 14, 2020, https://thepeachedtortilla.com/merchandise/cookbook

3. Andrew Chase, "Successful Food Truck Owners Fueled by Friendly Competition," *The Austinot* (blog), September 4, 2015, https://austinot.com/austin-food-trucks

4. ADL: Fighting Hate for Good, accessed October 17, 2020, https://www.adl.org/

5. Jeff Hyman, "Let's Toast the Holy Grail of Hiring," *Forbes*, January 30, 2019, https://www.forbes.com/sites/jeffhyman/2019/01/30/grail/#3d7964811ad5; Roy Maurer, "Employee Referrals Remain Top Source for Hires," SHRM (blog), June 23, 2017, https://www.shrm.org/resourcesandtools/hr-topics/talent-acquisition/pages/employee-referrals-remains-top-source-hires.aspx

6. Reid Hoffman, "How Large Is Your Network?" LinkedIn, December 6, 2012, https://www.linkedin.com/pulse/20121206195559-1213-how -large-is-your-network-the-power-of-2nd-and-3rd-degree-connections

7. Rick Hanson, "Common Ground," *Psychology Today* (blog), February 4, 2019, https://www.psychologytoday.com/us/blog/your-wise -brain/201902/common-ground

8. Robert F. Hurley, "The Decision to Trust," *Harvard Business Review*, September 2006, https://hbr.org/2006/09/the-decision-to-trust

9. Karyn Hall, "Create a Sense of Belonging," *Psychology Today* (blog), March 24, 2014, https://www.psychologytoday.com/us/blog/pieces -mind/201403/create-sense-belonging

10. Dwayne D. Gremler and Kevin P. Gwinner, "Rapport-Building Behaviors Used by Retail Employees," *Journal of Retailing* 84, no. 3 (2008): 308–324, http://citeseerx.ist.psu.edu/viewdoc /download?doi=10.1.1.456.3318&rep=rep1&type=pdf

11. Gremler and Gwinner, "Rapport-Building Behaviors," 310; referencing Gilbert A. Churchill, Robert H. Collins, and William A. Strang, "Should Retail Salespersons Be Similar to Their Customers?" *Journal of Retailing* 51 (Fall 1975): 29–44.

12. Gremler and Gwinner, "Rapport-Building Behaviors," 316; referencing Lawrence A. Crosby, Kenneth R. Evans, and Deborah Cowles, "Relationship Quality in Services Selling: An Interpersonal Influence Perspective," *Journal of Marketing* 54 (July 1990): 68–81.

13. Gremler and Gwinner, "Rapport-Building Behaviors," 310; referencing Daniel Goleman, "What Makes a Leader?" *Harvard Business Review* 76 (November–December 1998): 92–102.

14. "Daniel Goleman: What Ingredients to Build Rapport," Key Step Media, September 13, 2012, https://www.youtube.com /watch?v=uowxqr5N1YY; "Daniel Goleman's Five Components of Emotional Intelligence," https://web.sonoma.edu/users/s/swijtink /teaching/philosophy_101/paper1/goleman.htm

15. Karen Karbo, "Friendship: The Laws of Attraction," *Psychology Today*, last reviewed June 9, 2016, https://www.psychologytoday.com /us/articles/200611/friendship-the-laws-attraction

16. "2019 Horizon Report," Educause, https://library.educause.edu
    /resources/2019/4/2019-horizon-report

17. "What Is Appreciative Inquiry?" Center for Appreciative Inquiry,
    accessed October 14, 2020, https://www.centerforappreciativeinquiry
    .net/more-on-ai/what-is-appreciative-inquiry-ai

18. "The Knock Method™ – Interview #1: Why Move for Hunger
    Abandoned Cold-Calling," *TheRebeccammendations* (blog), June 2,
    2018, https://rebeccammendations.com/blog/2018/06/02/building
    -career-relationships-why-move-for-hunger-abandoned-cold-calling/

CHAPTER 5

1. *The Vegetarian Tourist* (blog), accessed October 14, 2020,
    http://www.vegetariantourist.com

2. "Malcolm Gladwell," Gladwell Books, accessed October 14, 2020,
    www.gladwellbooks.com

3. "Adam Grant: Organizational Psychologist and Bestselling Author,"
    Adam Grant.net, accessed October 14, 2020, www.adamgrant.net

4. Adam Grant, "What Makes Malcolm Gladwell Fascinating," LinkedIn,
    October 7, 2013, https://www.linkedin.com/pulse/20131007120010
    -69244073-what-makes-malcolm-gladwell-fascinating

5. Alex Soojung-Kim Pang, "How Resting More Can Boost Your
    Productivity," *Greater Good Magazine*, May 11, 2017, https://
    greatergood.berkeley.edu/article/item/how_resting_more_can_boost
    _your_productivity

6. Amy Rees Anderson, "The Fastest Way to Achieve Success Is to First
    Help Others Succeed," *Forbes*, January 6, 2016, https://www.forbes
    .com/sites/amyanderson/2016/01/06/the-fastest-way-to-achieve-success
    -is-to-first-help-others-succeed/#6ae456d179f9

7. "Helping Others Makes Us Happier At Work, Research Finds,"
    Huffington Post, July 30, 2013, https://www.huffpost.com/entry
    /helping-others-happy-altruism-work_n_3672477

8. "People's readiness to seek and receive help as affected by two basic
    psychological needs: the need for belongingness (Baumeister & Leary,
    1995), and the need for independence (Ryan & Deci, 2000). The

feeling of belongingness with others constitutes the psychological glue that makes social life possible. It is the basis of social solidarity that binds people in dyadic relationships and in groups (Reicher & Haslam, 2009). It is felt by almost all of us toward our close family members and by many of us toward larger groups, such as groups of co-workers and friends." Referencing Baumeister & Leary (1995), stating that "individuals possess a universal and fundamental 'need to belong'" (p. 3990). In Arie Nadler, "The Other Side of Helping: Seeking and Receiving Help," *The Oxford Handbook of Prosocial Behavior*, David A. Schroeder and William G. Graziano, eds. (London: Oxford University Press, 2015), 1, https://www.researchgate.net /publication/318876735_The_Other_Side_of_Helping_Seeking _and_Receiving_Help_of_a_single_chapter_of_a_title_in_Oxford _Handbooks_Online_for_personal_use_for_details_see_Privacy_Policy

9. "Seeking assistance may be associated [in people's minds] with an open admission of failure and dependence on others. These anticipated psychological costs often hinder the seeking of help, which may result in the intensification of the problem (Nadler, 1991)." Arie Nadler, "Personality and Help Seeking," in G.R. Pierce, B. Lakey, I.G. Sarason, and B.R. Sarason, eds., *Sourcebook of Social Support and Personality. The Springer Series in Social/Clinical Psychology* (Boston: Springer, 1997), https://doi.org/10.1007/978-1-4899-1843-7_17

10. Tammy D. Allen and Lillian T. Eby, "Common Bonds: An Integrative View of Mentoring Relationships," *The Blackwell Handbook of Mentoring: A Multiple Perspectives Approach* (Hoboken, NY: Wiley-Blackwell, 2010), 397–419.

11. "An effective mentorship fulfills the 'need to belong, or form and maintain positive interpersonal relationships with others, which is fulfilled through affiliation and acceptance from others' (Gardner, Picket & Brewer, 2000)." In Allen and Eby, "Common Bonds," 399.

12. Year Up, accessed October 14, 2020, https://www.yearup.org

13. "Avoiding Early Match Termination," Mentoring Fact Sheet, U.S. Department of Education Mentoring Resource Center, July 2007, https:// educationnorthwest.org/sites/default/files/resources/factsheet18.pdf

14. Worline and Dutton, *Awakening Compassion*, 5.

15. A. Edmondson, "Psychological Safety and Learning Behaviour in Work
     Teams," *Administrative Science Quarterly* 44, no. 2 (1999): 350; Harry
     Kaloudis, "Psychological Safety at Work," *Medium*, March 18, 2019,
     https://medium.com/@Harri_Kaloudis/psychological-safety-at-work
     -what-do-psychologically-safe-work-teams-look-like-5585ab0f2df4

16. Sara L. Rynes, Jean M. Bartunek, Jane E. Dutton, and Joshua D.
     Margolis, "Care and Compassion Through an Organizational Lens:
     Opening Up New Possibilities," *The Academy of Management Review*
     37, no. 4 (October 2012): 503–523, https://www.researchgate
     .net/publication/235964708_Care_and_Compassion_Through_an
     _Organizational_Lens_Opening_Up_New_Possibilities

17. Rynes, Bartunek, Dutton, Margolis, "Care and Compassion Through
     an Organizational Lens."

18. Worline and Dutton, *Awakening Compassion*, 15.

19. Ron Carucci, "How to Overcome Your Obsession with Helping
     Others," *Harvard Business Review*, February 18, 2020, https://hbr
     .org/2020/02/how-to-overcome-your-obsession-with-helping-others

20. "How to Create an Annual Giving Plan," *TheRebeccammendations*
     (blog), March 23, 2018, https://rebeccammendations.com
     /blog/2018/03/26/how-to-create-an-annual-giving-plan

21. Year Up, accessed October 14, 2020, https://www.yearup.org/

22. Move for Hunger, accessed October 14, 2020, https://moveforhunger.org/

23. Twist Out Cancer, accessed October 14, 2020, https://twistoutcancer.org/

24. Alex Wood, Deepak Chopra, Paul J. Mills, et al., "The Role of
     Gratitude in Spiritual Well-Being in Asymptomatic Heart Failure
     Patients," *Spirituality in Clinical Practice* 2, no. 1 (2015): 5–17, https://
     www.apa.org/pubs/journals/releases/scp-0000050.pdf; Jeff C. Huffman,
     Eleanor E. Beale, Christopher M. Celano, et al., "Effects of Optimism
     and Gratitude on Physical Activity, Biomarkers, and Readmissions
     After an Acute Coronary Syndrome," *Circulation: Cardiovascular
     Quality and Outcomes* 9 (2016): 55–63, https://www.ahajournals.org
     /doi/full/10.1161/CIRCOUTCOMES.115.002184

25. Kori D. Miller, "14 Health Benefits of Practicing Gratitude According to Science," PositivePsychology.com, January 9, 2020, https://positivepsychology.com/benefits-of-gratitude

WRAP UP: KEEP ON KNOCKING

1. Chase, "Successful Food Truck Owners."

2. "Intelligent Online Appointment Scheduling," Time Trade, accessed October 14, 2020, http://www.timetrade.com

3. Calendly, accessed October 14, 2020, http://www.calendly.com

4. Courtney E. Ackerman, "Gratitude Journal: A Collection of 67 Templates, Ideas, and Apps for Your Diary," PositivePsychology.com, September 18, 2020, https://positivepsychology.com/gratitude-journal

5. The Knock Method, accessed October 14, 2020, http://www.theknockmethod.com

6. Ibid.

ACKNOWLEDGMENTS

There was no way I was writing a whole chapter about giving and gratitude without thanking the many, many individuals who have stood behind me, and with me, and are waiting up ahead to help make this book a success!

Six years. "Why haven't I finished this book yet?" This thought came into my mind many times during that time, accompanied by feelings of embarrassment and doubt. I now realize six years was exactly what I needed to live challenging and rewarding career and life experiences, cross paths with the right mix of humans, and harmonize their brain power, generosity, compassion, and craft. Some of their stories—and mine—and research in this book wouldn't have been ready to share had they not been given the time to percolate, manifest, and flourish. To all of those who listened to my book concept; agreed to an interview; generously shared your stories, advice, and knowledge; attended a workshop; shared an idea; cheered me on; and helped this book come to life, thank you.

In 2016, when my husband, Ross, and I were newly dating, we sat in the Vancouver restaurant Forage, and in the dim lighting, I told him about my in-progress book and my aspirations to finish it. This wasn't the only out-there idea I shared with him—I, and we, conjure up new ventures all the time. The good ones stick. Four years later, I'm writing these acknowledgments, and he has been my constant through it all. To the one I admire, adore, and love with all my heart, Ross, thank you for listening, being critical where it counts, debating subtitles and regional phrases, balancing me out, brainstorming concluding chapters on summer hikes, giving advice about researching publishers that led me to my amazing editor, and for humoring all of my ideas—strengthening the intriguing ones and helping me admit to the leave-behinds. I eagerly await what *our* ideas become. I love you.

To my parents, Leslie and Rick, I am grateful for the example you set for my sisters and me to work hard for what's important. Because the business you built served small and local business owners whose success and family were deeply intertwined, like yours, you taught me to think about the human aspect of business. Thank you for supporting and encouraging all of my educational and professional experiences, even when that meant studying abroad in Spain, hosting my blog's first birthday party, picking up and moving to Chicago, and leaving the corporate world to start a business at twenty-six. You've trusted these bold moves, and your faith in me has carried me through it all. And thank you for reading my draft chapters in record time because of your excitement to dive into my words, stories, and ideas. Dad, thank you for exemplifying that you can connect with just about anyone, whether in line at the coffee shop, with a customer service rep on the phone, or, of course, with your family. Your stories in this book demonstrate how adding a little human touch, and a little touch of humor, to career interactions makes business more personal and drives career success.

To my sisters, Julie and Allyson, thank you for being an ear, a shoulder, an idea bank. You are the ones I go to to be myself and be understood. You're both creative in your own ways, and I'm thankful that your creativity has rubbed off on me, even if I'm a little too punny. Allyson, thank you for designing the very first workbook for The Knock Method workshops and The Knock Method logo, which gave this career development educational program credibility and made it more official, and for being my go-to design consultant.

To Grandma Joyce, I think my creativity comes partly from you. While I'm not the painter that you are, we have always connected on creative outlets, and you are always eager to hear about how my writing is going. Thank you for your support and encouragement for all of my endeavors, whether the blog post I wrote on your birthday years ago or this book.

To my in-laws, Mark and Sue, thank you for supporting Ross's and my endeavors, including this book. Mark, thank you for connecting me to other writers and editors, which gave me encouragement about this long, winding process.

Speaking of family, to my cousin Yosi Finn, thank you for being so generous with your guidance, from helping me file my first trademark on my own when I started my blog over ten years ago, to being a sounding board as my original content in this book came to life with my publisher. Your intellectual property expertise, coupled with your care and generosity to help me as a family member and client, has provided me with the reassurance I needed as I put my ideas in print out into the world. Thank you.

They say good things are worth the wait, and so are good people. It took me almost a year to find my irreplaceable editor, Josh Bernoff, and a nice stretch of time after that first conversation to prove that I had the stories that my readers were waiting for and the drive to put in the work. Josh, once we partnered up, you assured me that my message was worthy of a book, and your opinion fueled my perseverance and confidence. Your ability to coach (which you love so much) is admirable—for one, you broke down my defensive walls, which my family can attest is no easy feat, and two, instead of writing and fixing for me, you taught me lasting writing strategies and improved my writing ability exponentially (I hope my readers will agree). You always had a suggestion or solution for every doubt or question I brought to you. Can you solve all of my life challenges? Don't worry, I'll never stop using the word "shared" entirely (I'm too collaborative to leave it out), or packing too many words into sentences. But I will end sentences sooner. And then build on them. I am so grateful to you for believing in me, and for our friendship that has emerged through our working relationship—that's what The Knock Method is all about, right?

To Tanya Hall, the CEO of Greenleaf Book Group, thank you for giving me and my book a chance, fifteen years after my internship during college. Your passion translates to believing in new and established authors, and your belief in me made the difference between my having an idea and my having a book that has the power to build confidence and build career relationships that change the course of my readers' lives. To Lindsey Clark, my lead editor at Greenleaf, thank you for making the time to get to know me and my ideas. Your unconditional support and ability to honor my voice and experience as-is has been only positive from the day we met, and I am so grateful for your ideas on weaving in more creativity and personal voice. Thank you also for helping me realize my book is a book (pinch me!). To Jen Glynn, thank you for keeping our project on track, and the team focused. To Daniel Sandoval, your positivity and openness to my ideas on how to make my book come to life in a way that is truly representative of what I believe in helped make my dream a reality. And your patience in answering all of my questions and supportive solutions that make *Knock* an ecoconscious (paperback cover), authentic (like Step 3), and collaborative work (accommodating the editor I brought to the team) means more to me than you know. To Judy Marchman and Pam Nordberg, thank you for your detailed editing eyes and for working to retain both my voice and accuracy in my words. To Chase Quarterman, thank you for bringing a fun, bright, and slightly out-there design to this book cover. Your openness to my ideas and reassurance as it came together made this most fun part of seeing my book come to life even more fulfilling! To the entire Greenleaf team—you make the publishing industry's reputation for being tough, inflexible, and sometimes untouchable melt away, and for providing me a channel to put my ideas out into the world to help others with nothing but a positive experience, I thank you. Thank you for giving me a chance as a first-time author, and turning our one-time interaction when I was a college intern fifteen years ago into a long-term, mutually beneficial career relationship.

To Kelly Nash Vedas, Adam Vedas, Dan Rosenstein, Ryan Zieman, and Carly Schlafer, thank you for supporting The Knock Method from the start—whether through attending the very first workshop or inviting me to host or co-host a workshop, you provided me with valuable learning experiences and feedback that shaped the book, and you were supporters and early adopters of just a spark of an idea.

To Samantha Adams, beyond an insightful and empowering interview you agreed to have with me one weeknight close to midnight for the book, you have supported this book endeavor in myriad ways. You reviewed my writing when the concept was just budding nearly six years before it was published. You always asked excitedly about my book's progress and encouraged me to keep going. You helped me find the internship in college at Greenleaf Book Group in 2005 when we were merely college sophomores, which led to them publishing this book fifteen years later. Thank you for inspiring me through your writing, work, and kismet-y friendship.

To Sarah Rosner, Brie Gorlitsky, and Matt Weiner, thank you for your encouragement. Whether expressing excitement to buy one of the first copies, sharing the trials and tribulations of finding your creative groove or the realities of writer's (or songwriter's) block, or kicking around ideas for how The Knock Method readers can connect live, beyond the pages of this book, you've all helped make it happen. Brie, I wish I had a dollar for every time you said, "You can put this in your book." I hope I've done all of our career and life conversations justice because I'm pretty sure we have an anthology to write with all of the material we have collected over the years.

To Nikki Keidan, thank you for always being my cheerleader, even for things I didn't know were cheer-worthy! I learn so much from your stick-to-it-iveness (I'm still in shock that you tore up that check that I gave you), your negotiating skills, and your dedicated friendship. I'm so lucky to have you in my corner, and I'm always in yours.

To Batami Baskin, thank you for reading a draft chapter, taking a sneak peek at the cover, and for your candid feedback. I know I can always count on you to sugarcoat your opinion.

To Sapna Dalal, thank you for your encouragement and excitement for me to tell the story of how we met. It really was meant to be, and I admire your adventurous, humorous, and generous spirit. I can't wait to share more ideas with each other and support each other's future endeavors. Now, go make some juice!

To Ben Cecil, thank you for being the first and only almost-client I ever cried with. You have the ability to look beyond personal needs and think outside the box, and you are an expert in your craft. Thank you for partnering to make an impact on small businesses, even when it didn't make too much business sense financially. The Austin Video Marketing Marathon was epic, and it demonstrated the collective power high-quality career relationships can have. I think it's time for a new project, eh?

To Dafna Michaelson Jenet, thank you for your openness. Thank you for representing not only your constituency but your community. Your willingness to give, give, give makes an impact beyond what can be put on paper. And, your ability to connect, whether on public social issues or personal grief and resilience, is refreshing and cherished.

To Kathy Hardy, thank you for believing in the power of career development education for young professionals and The Knock Method. Thank you for helping me secure a key interview for the book to inspire effective mentoring practices.

To my mentor, Adam Hanin, thank you for being my sounding board and advocate. Over three years, we've formed a friendship, and I am grateful for the opportunity to share career and life experiences without judgment and, instead, with positive reinforcement. Thank you for exemplifying a high-quality career relationship in the form of mentorship that I, and my readers, can learn from.

To my work manager, Ben Stein, thank you for exemplifying compassion at work, an important aspect of building high-quality career relationships that this book encourages, especially during one of the most difficult times in my life.

To Joan Yanabu, my work team's leader, I have learned so much working with you, and I so value your encouragement and support at work and personally. Thank you for your confidence in me and the opportunity to establish and nurture high-quality relationships among our internal teams to strengthen our customer impact. There is exactly one VP I've ever cried with, and that was you, and your ability to put work aside to express human compassion is what building high-quality career relationships is all about. Thank you.

To Jamie Domenici, former Salesforce Customer Success Adoption & Growth team leader, thank you for your support of my personal project, and for investing in our partnership work across the company to achieve the optimal, most impactful connected digital customer experience.

To Tricia Austin, thank you for exemplifying what it means to put people first, at work and beyond. You give my readers and me confidence through the fact that we established our high-quality career relationship after I didn't get the job on your team. You still made time to provide me with feedback, and that led to a broader conversation about career and our Austin commonality, and I am grateful to work with you and to know you. Thank you for helping me share my ideas and passion for career development within our company—your guidance led to several important conversations and approvals that helped this book come to life. Thank you.

To Tiffani Bova, thank you for taking the time to mentor new authors like myself, and demonstrate how to live your values. I appreciate each conversation we have. Your advice and guidance elevate my confidence that as an author, our personal and professional brands can coexist and complement each other to maximize impact for others, also leading to a more fulfilling life. Keep putting your ideas out into the universe—the world is better for it!

To Jenn Beatty, thank you for taking the time to meet with me on Adam's request. Your advice led me to important research and a new high-quality career relationship with Dr. Jane Dutton, which has been empowering, eye-opening, and life-enriching.

To Adam Grant, you are a vision and an inspiration, not just for me, but for quality connectors everywhere (well, it seems like everywhere!). Thank you for bringing science and research to the workplace and lives of so many to deepen the way we connect with others. Your ability to make intricate concepts relatable and universally understood is unmatched. Thank you for your generosity in sharing your advice about the myriad ways we can help others, and for opening the door when I reached out, resulting in a late-night phone interview on a rainy night when your plane was delayed to Chicago, a quick meeting at Chicago Ideas Week the next day, and an ongoing dialogue about your insights that have already impacted so many students and professionals through The Knock Method workshops. I can't wait for *Knock* readers to go behind the scenes to learn how you and Malcolm formed a high-quality career connection that keeps giving beyond you two.

To Dr. Jane Dutton, who knew that when I reached out to have a conversation about your research and writing on compassion in the workplace, that a new high-quality career relationship would emerge? We have never met, yet I feel close to you. You have a way with words and human connection, and after such an accomplished career, your passion to nurture and lift up others like myself is unmatched. Your feedback changed the course of my writing and reshaped my ideas. Because of you, I carry a responsibility to shift conversations from "me" to "you" and "us," and to help others do the same, not just because it feels good, leads to positive outcomes, and is healthier for us, but because it is critical for a future that is caring, productive, progressive, and safe. Thank you for making the time to get to know me and truly invest in my work (as if you needed yet another student to teach!). You showed my readers and me that people will make time to invest in high-quality career and human relationships, regardless of geography, experience level, title, or competing priorities, if it creates value and puts goodness into the world.

To those whose stories, research, and hard-earned advice are included in these pages and support The Knock Method with proof and inspiration, thank you: Rick Otis, Adam Grant, Jane Dutton, Eric Silverstein, Jessica Malkin, Julie Smolyansky, Adam Lowy, Jenna Benn Shersher, Erica Kuhl, Gerald Chertavian, Andy Crestodina, Jennifer Levine, and Jeff Aeder. Your openness, generosity, vulnerability, and success most certainly give me the reassurance and confidence—as it will for *career growers*, *career changers*, and *career builders*—that we can build positive, high-quality, mutually beneficial career relationships as we develop our careers and build bridges to a stronger, more impactful community that will shape the future for all of us.

INDEX

ABOUT THE AUTHOR

REBECCA OTIS LEDER unlocks the power of human connection wherever she goes. While her resume says she's a cross-channel marketer, that's just part of the story—she builds relationships, community, and learning opportunities for companies, organizations, and people with a unique offering or mission.

Rebecca is a career educator, an instructional designer and facilitator of professional development workshops that help organizations cultivate a culture of connection. She also serves as a strategic advisor for companies large and small focused on innovative workforce and talent development learning experiences where individuals create meaningful careers through high-quality relationship building strategies.

Rebecca was a senior manager at Salesforce, where she brought more than one hundred employees together from two distinct internal teams by uncovering and combining their unique strengths to create training apps that helped more than fifteen thousand customers. Rebecca has shared her career development, personal branding, and marketing insights for companies, classrooms, and conferences spanning financial services, media, hospitality, nonprofit, higher education, and tech industries, including Salesforce, Amazon, Goldman Sachs 10,000 Small Businesses, DePaul and Loyola universities, Startup Institute Chicago, BlogHer, JewishColorado, Silicon Valley Jewish High Tech Community, and Year Up.

Rebecca established the first social media policies for the state of Texas at Texas.gov in 2010 (she Tweeted for Texas!), and she authored an award-winning entertainment blog, *TheRebeccammendations*. At the age of twenty-six, she was named a Rising Star Finalist in the 2012 *Austin Business Journal* Women of Influence awards after founding a successful small-business marketing consultancy, helping more than twenty-five local businesses, startups, and nonprofits reach new audiences. Now, Rebecca has distilled the culmination of her dynamic career into five actionable steps, known as The Knock Method, to fill a confidence and education gap so that *career growers*, *career builders*, and *career changers* not only have the tools but feel empowered to build high-quality, mutually beneficial career relationships that don't just lead to jobs, but strengthen our collective power to drive change.

The Knock Method has been featured by *Fast Company, Inc. Magazine*, Silicon Republic, NPR, Thrive Global, and national news stations, including in Austin, Chicago, Denver, El Paso, Portland, and Washington D. C.